THE SIT
23529 BEVERLY
ST. CLAIR SHORES, MICH. 48082

THE KENTUCKY RIFLE

THE KENTUCKY RIFLE

by MERRILL LINDSAY

Photographs by BRUCE PENDLETON

Arma Press · The Historical Society of York County

Published by Arma Press / The Historical Society of York County

Arma Press
160 Sixth Avenue, New York, N.Y. 10013

Copyright © 1972 by Merrill Lindsay
All rights reserved

Library of Congress Catalogue Card Number LC-72-78520
I.S.B.N. Cloth 8079-0185-7

2nd printing

Printed and bound in Italy.

Table of Contents

Where Did the Name Come From?
Introduction: The Aesthetics of the Kentucky Rifle
1. Pre-Revolutionary
2. The Lancaster School
3. The Bethlehem School
4. The Reading School
5. The Associated Bethlehem School
6. The Lebanon School
7. The Dauphin School
8. The York School
9. The Littlestown School
10. The Emmitsburg School
11. The Chambersburg School
12. The Bedford School
13. The Maryland School
14. The Virginia School
15. The North Carolina School
16. Regional
17. The Mechanism of the Kentucky
18. Silver Mounted Kentucky Rifles
19. A Kentucky Garniture
20. Kentucky Pistols
21. List of Gunsmiths

Where Did the Name Come From?

Following the American victory at the Battle of New Orleans, substantially won by the Kentucky rifle in the hands of about two thousand frontiersmen from Kentucky, a ballad, "The Hunters of Kentucky," was written. It dramatized the exploits of these undisciplined riflemen who defeated the military might of England.

The ballad became widely popular throughout the new nation, so much so that the version sung at the Chatham Garden Theatre in New York City was published in the form of sheet music by George Willig in Philadelphia. Popular songs stayed around for several years in those days. The popularity of this ballad lasted long enough to be translated into Pennsylvania German before it had run its course.

At the Chatham Garden, the song, with words by S. Woodworth accompanying music by William Blondell, was "sung in character" by a Mr. Petrie. This early star of musical comedy is pictured on the sheet music in his role as a Kentucky rifleman. He is wearing a fringed bathrobe-like garment gathered in the front by a sash with tassels. Fringed stovepipe pants cover his boot tops. A fringed scarf or cape is draped over his shoulders and on top of Mr. Petrie's head there is a huge cossack shaped beaver hat with a tiny brim. Despite the actor's laughable appearance as a frontiersman, he and his song were greeted "with unbounded applause," at least, according to the puff on the song sheet.

In the fifth stanza of the lyrics, the Kentucky rifle received its name which was to stay with it from that time on. The expression "Kentucky rifle" became one of those singular examples of a designation documented in its own period.

> "But Jackson he was wide awake and wasn't scar'd at trifles
> For well he knew what aim we take, with our KENTUCKY RIFLES,
> So he led us down to Cypress Swamp, the ground was low and Mucky,
> There stood John Bull in martial pomp but here was old Kentucky."

The frontiersmen who went to Kentucky and on into the Louisiana Territory bought and brought their rifles from Pennsylvania, Maryland and Virginia but chiefly from Pennsylvania. The Pennsylvania towns along the roads leading to the West are remembered as the locations of the schools of rifle design.

There were few, if any, Kentucky rifles made in Kentucky, although there were some Kentuckys made in Tennessee, Ohio and Indiana. By the time that manufacturing and metal work was being done west of Pittsburgh, the demand of the frontiersman was for Plains rifles. Stubby, large bore half-stocked saddle guns took the place of the long, graceful flintlock gun which had fed and protected the rifleman as he made his lonely way over the Appalachian trails to the grasslands of Kentucky.

The Aesthetics of the Kentucky Rifle

The beauty of a Greek helmet or a suit of gothic armor lies in its simplicity. The smooth, uncluttered lines of both derive from the intended function of the piece. Kentucky rifles derive their beauty from their severe adherence to functional line and proportion. The proportion to each other of the elements of the gun: the stock, the throat, the barrel length and the fore end, as well as the amount of drop of the stock, the cast-off to the right from breech to butt, the straight, convex or concave profile lines of the stock, the thickness of the stock at the butt and throat, the use of carved mouldings in the wood to accent the shape, the cameo cuttings which visually separate the throat from the stock and finally the shape and extent of the cheek piece are summed up in one word. That word is architecture.

After an early experimental period between 1710 and 1740, while features of the heavy, accurate German Jaeger's rifle were combined with the longer and more graceful French and British long fowlers, there emerged a truly original object of American craft, the Kentucky rifle. In the brief history of the European colonies in America, the Kentucky rifle may well be considered the outstanding indigenous art form.

The effectiveness of the Kentucky as a well-designed tool made it a cherished object to its owners, who depended upon it for both food and protection. Thus, as a possession of real value, it became the recipient of decoration which reflected its worth. Wooden patch boxes were replaced with ornate brass patch boxes often consisting of three or four pieces whose graceful curves and cutouts were inlaid in the curly maple stocks, and the surface decorated with burin-cut C-scrolls and other elements of rococco design. Plain wooden stocks or utilitarian stocks favored with simple incised scratching of more rococo "C" and tendril borders were supplanted with fine relief carving worthy of the best Philadelphia, New York or Boston cabinet work of the period. Unornamented fore ends and cheek pieces were accented with silver and brass inlays whose sometime function as retainers of barrel pins was secondary to their display value and indication of their owner's enthusiasms and interests.

This second phase, just described, has been called by Kentucky expert, Joe Kindig, "the golden age of the Kentucky rifle." "It was during this period after the Revolutionary War that the patch box began to acquire a beauty through rococo design which made it the outstanding element of the Kentucky rifle and a purely American innovation worthy of being considered a work of art."

The third era of the Kentucky rifle starts with the beginning of the percussion period and ends with the introduction of breech-loading cartridge guns. The architecture-toward-function tended to be ignored. For economic reasons and ease of manufacture the stocks became thinner, flatter and more board shaped. The deep relief carving was replaced by an elaboration of flat brass and silver inlays whose presence identifies them with the late Federal and early Victorian décor.

Again we find a parallel in the comparison of degenerate

Roman sculpture to the classic Greek originals; in the gilded, engraved, slashed and embossed parade armor of the seventeenth century as compared to the aesthetically pleasing smooth surfaces of the lance deflecting armor of the sixteenth. In one case, the art is the object itself; in the other, the object becomes secondary while the surface provides a canvas to be decorated.

This simple description does not explain the mystique of the Kentucky. Collectors admire and appreciate Kentucky rifles for far more than what they can see, touch or explain. This may be because the gun is uniquely American, part of the heritage of the American male. It may also stem from the collective inherited memory of the time when the American long rifle was a secret weapon and a psychological strength to a little band of revolutionaries who had all too few real weapons with which to defend themselves.

It is also a triumph of singlehanded craftsmanship. Where these skills came from no one seems to know. The German gunsmiths who came to Pennsylvania had no heritage which trained them to make a complete gun. They came from a land of crafts and guilds where they had been apprenticed as barrel makers, locksmiths, woodcarvers, engravers or steel carvers, stockmakers and assemblers. In the frontier towns of Pennsylvania, Maryland and Virginia they built, rifled, carved and assembled complete Kentucky rifles. They even engraved and decorated their own patch boxes and silver and brass inlays. Often the skills and the artistic perceptions which they exhibited were of a higher order than that of the contemporary silversmiths, engravers and cabinetmakers in their own communities, and rivalled the best work of skilled specialized craftsmen in the seaboard cities.

We don't know how these country blacksmiths became the artists that they were. All we know is that superb examples of their work exists. Here is a selection of the finest pieces made between 1760 and 1860. They are illustrated according to period and in groups or schools revealing the characteristic architecture and embellishment which distinguish the different areas and makers. The guns shown here are the best examples from the collections of individuals and museums all over the United States. They were brought together through the planning and knowledge of Joe Kindig, Jr., who did not live to see the show. The Historical Society of York County Museum, where the exhibition was held, The Kentucky Rifle Association, Joe's son, Joe III, and the collectors who parted temporarily with their treasures to make the show possible, all combined to produce a truly unique exhibition of indigenous American art. The highlights are reproduced on these pages.

EUROPEAN INFLUENCES

The Kentucky rifle evolved from two basic types: the long, light and graceful smoothbore fowling piece developed primarily by the English and French and the short, large calibre, rifled "Jaeger" developed by the huntsman of central Europe. This successful wedding of these two distinctly different types produced the long, graceful and highly accurate Kentucky rifle. It combined the beautiful architectural elements of the English fowler with the general ornamental features of the Jaeger; that is, the carving around the tang, the cheek piece and the functional sliding wooden cover over the box in the buttstock of the rifle. The latter eventually became the patch box of the Kentucky designed to hold the greased patches essential to its operation and aesthetically became the artistic focal point of the rifle. Technically, the Kentucky was the final phase in the three-hundred-year evolution of the muzzle-loading rifle.

SCHOOLS

When within any highly cultivated artistic center, craftsmen independently pursue their particular trade, working as creative individuals but develop styles or designs that are expressive of that center as a whole, their cumulative efforts are referred to as "a school." Thus Colonial America as it grew in cultural stature during the 18th century developed many rather sophisticated centers, areas of concentration of artistic talent in the overall field of the decorative arts. Possibly the greatest of these was the city of Philadelphia during the Queen Anne and Chippendale periods where the highly fashionable rococo designs of France and England reached their zenith in the colonies.

In the case of the Kentucky rifle, the sophisticated definition of "school" is set aside for one that is more workable. It refers to a geographical area within which there is a concentration of gunsmiths exchanging ideas. When the journeyman or apprentice of one school or area moved to another area a new school was born or an existing area was influenced. It was far less static artistically than the formal sense of schools in the metropolitan areas and permitted a greater freedom of expression. The actual geographical borders between these provincial schools was never sharply defined, but by presenting the majority of the Kentucky rifles in this exhibit in the context of their schools, the student is given a scholarly exposure to the influence of the individual gunsmith on his own school as well as the school's influence on other areas where it is applicable.

In tracing the artistic movement of these early gunsmiths as they slowly evolved this original and native art form we follow the movement of our growing nation westward. The purpose of this book is to bring together a very selective number of Kentucky rifles representative of the work of the more creative gunsmiths of the 18th and 19th centuries in order that the artistic originality of these rurally isolated artists may be recognized and appreciated as a major contribution to America's cultural heritage.

1. Pre-Revolutionary

The earliest Kentucky rifles quite naturally reflect the embryonic phase of the rifle's development. The early gunsmith is combining elements for the first time and is feeling his way through to the basic architecture of his rifle. The rifle at this stage precludes any extensive ornamentation, for the primary concern is one of production to supply the needs of the rapidly growing population. Simplicity becomes the rule. It was this concentration on line and proportion that eventually established the basic components essential for the rifle to blossom out fully in the Golden Age.

The patch boxes on the early examples were generally of wood and were purely functional, occasionally relieved with simple details of moulding. Contemporary with the wooden lid was the early American innovation of the simple two part brass patch box consisting of a head and hinged lid.

Overleaf full length, top to bottom:

1. JOHN SCHREIT 1761 (signed and dated on barrel). Reading, Pa.
John Schreit's rifle is the earliest dated Kentucky that we know of. The workmanship is of high order. The furniture is engraved, from the chevron grooving on the muzzle cap to the butt plate. A few, but not many early Reading and Lancaster rifles employ the chevron design. Length overall 58¾ in., bbl. 43 $\frac{5}{16}$ in., .52 cal., rifled.

2. JOHN SCHNEIDER / Mr. 19th 1776 (on the patch box lid). Location unknown.
The outstanding features of this Kentucky are the inscription on the typical two-piece patch box and the ivory inlays. There is a tapered ivory inlay on the underside of the stock and an ivory edge to the cheek piece. The use of ivory inlays is unusual on American long rifles. The stock has been relief carved and incised. Traces of the decorative carving are visible around the patch box. Length overall 62½ in., bbl. 47¾ in., .58 cal., smoothbore.

3. UNSIGNED. Attributed to the Reading area.
This Kentucky, the longest of the three pieces, may have been given this additional length to make it a more accurate target rifle. It is a simple handsome arm with its plain sliding patch box lid rubbed and polished smooth through years of use. The now darkened stock was made of curly maple, the favorite wood of the gunsmiths in Pennsylvania. Length overall 64¾ in., bbl. 50¾ in., .52 cal., rifled.

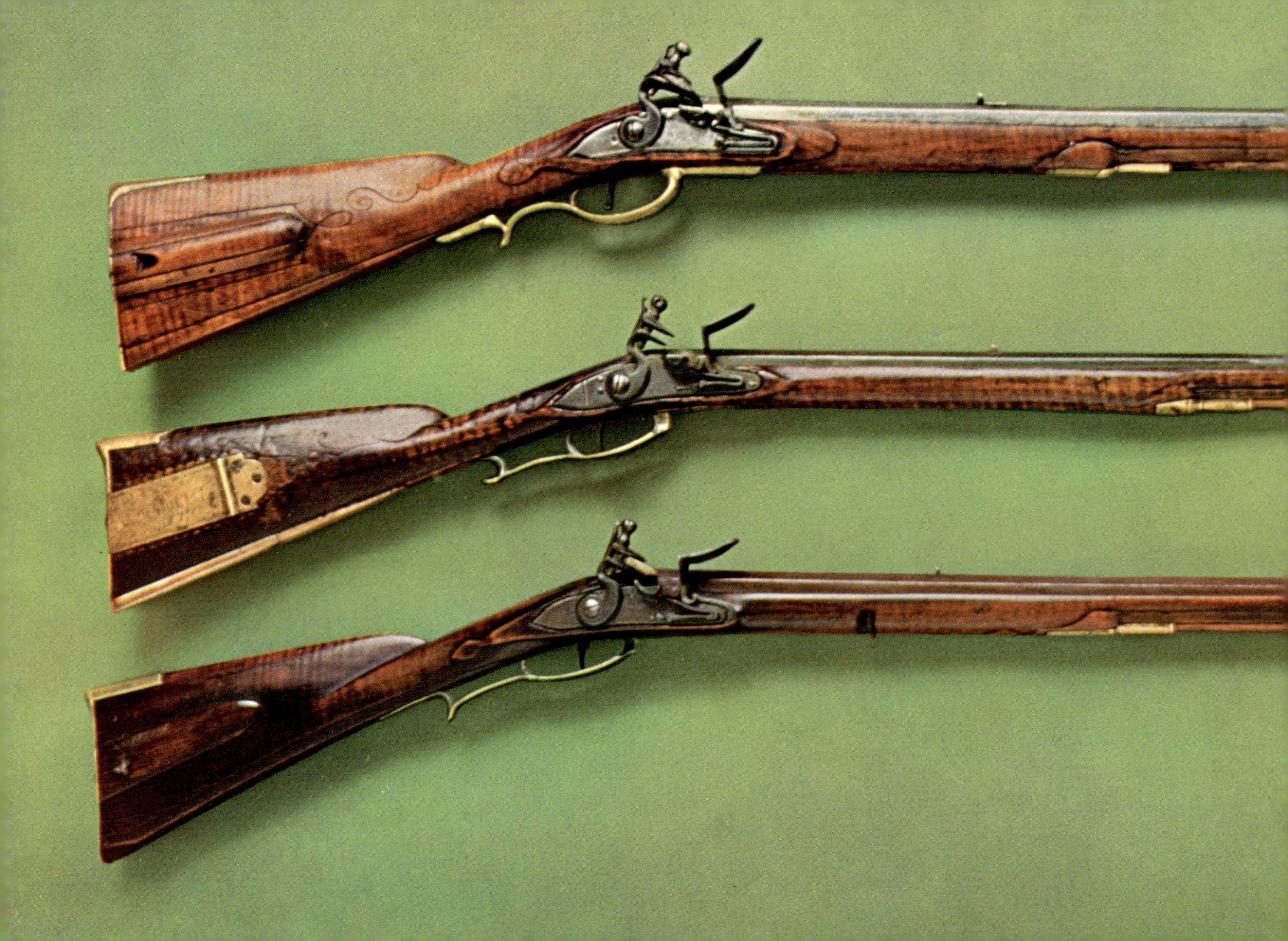

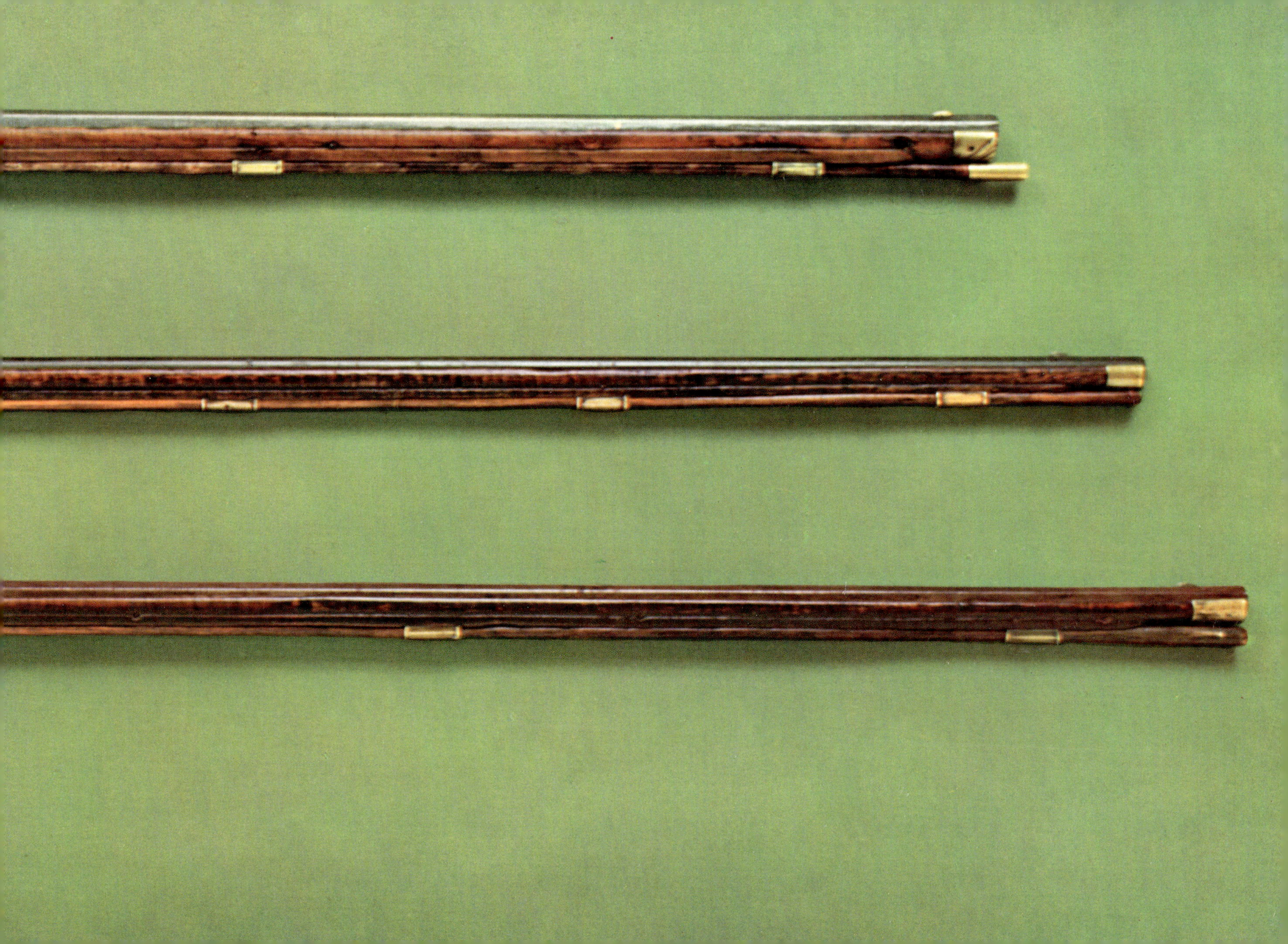

Right: Detail of left sides—cheek pieces of Nos. 1 & 4 to illustrate the evolution from incised carving to relief carved rococo "C".

Top: 1. JOHN SCHREIT, note the engraved side plate and butt plate return.

Bottom: 4. UNSIGNED. Attributed to John Philip Beck, who worked from the late 1760s until his death in 1811. Lebanon, Pa.

Beck rifles are carved in beautifully designed and well executed high relief. Kentucky experts Sam Dyke and Joe Kindig, Jr. considered J. P. Beck to be one of the greatest of the early gunsmiths of Pennsylvania and a truly masterful woodworker. The style of this arm—its architecture and relief carving—date it somewhere before 1780 although the formal rococo brass engraving on the trigger guard derive from a still earlier period. Length overall 56½ in., bbl. 40¾ in., .67 cal., smoothbore.

Left: Detail of inscription on patch box of No. 2.

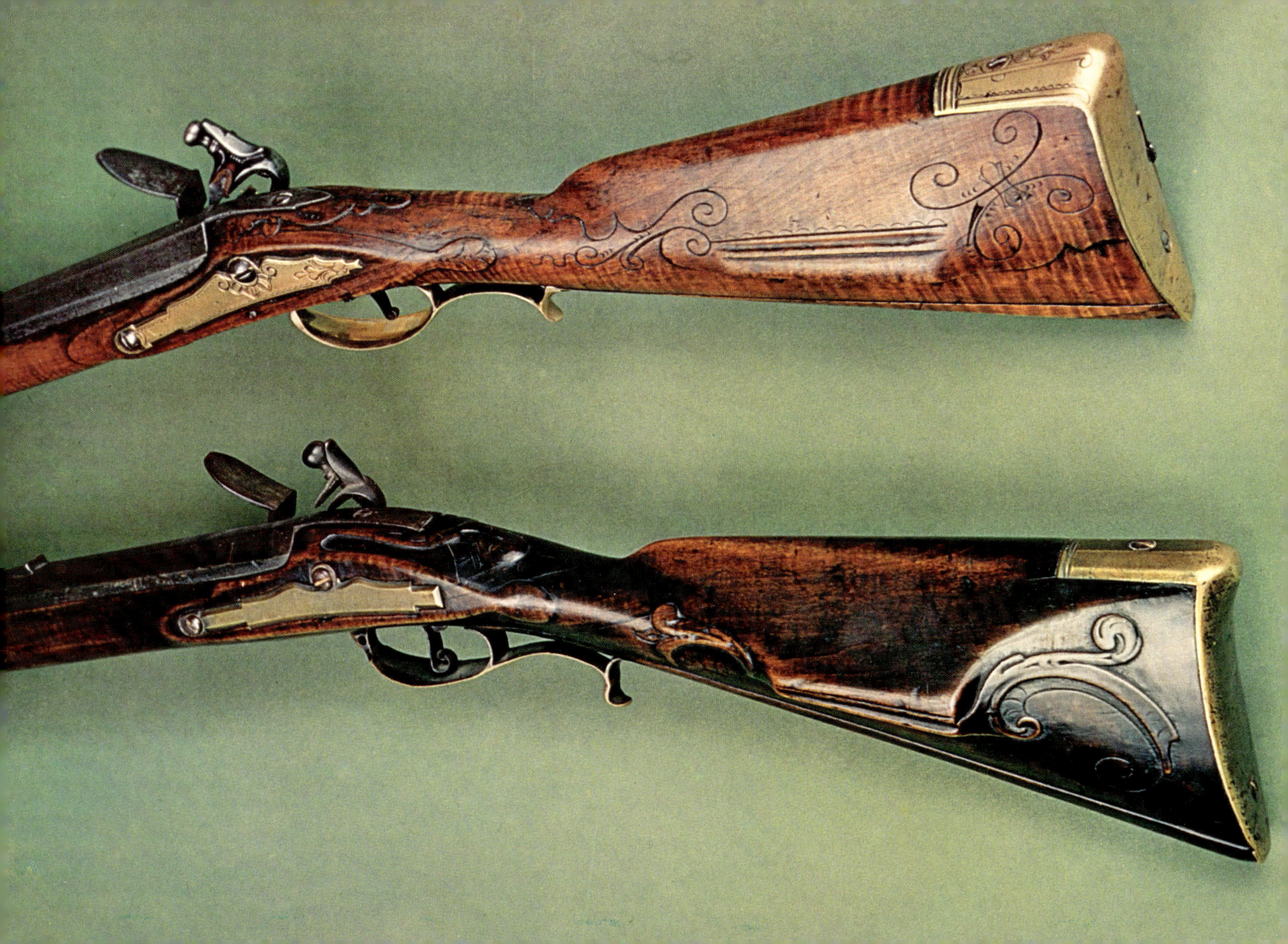

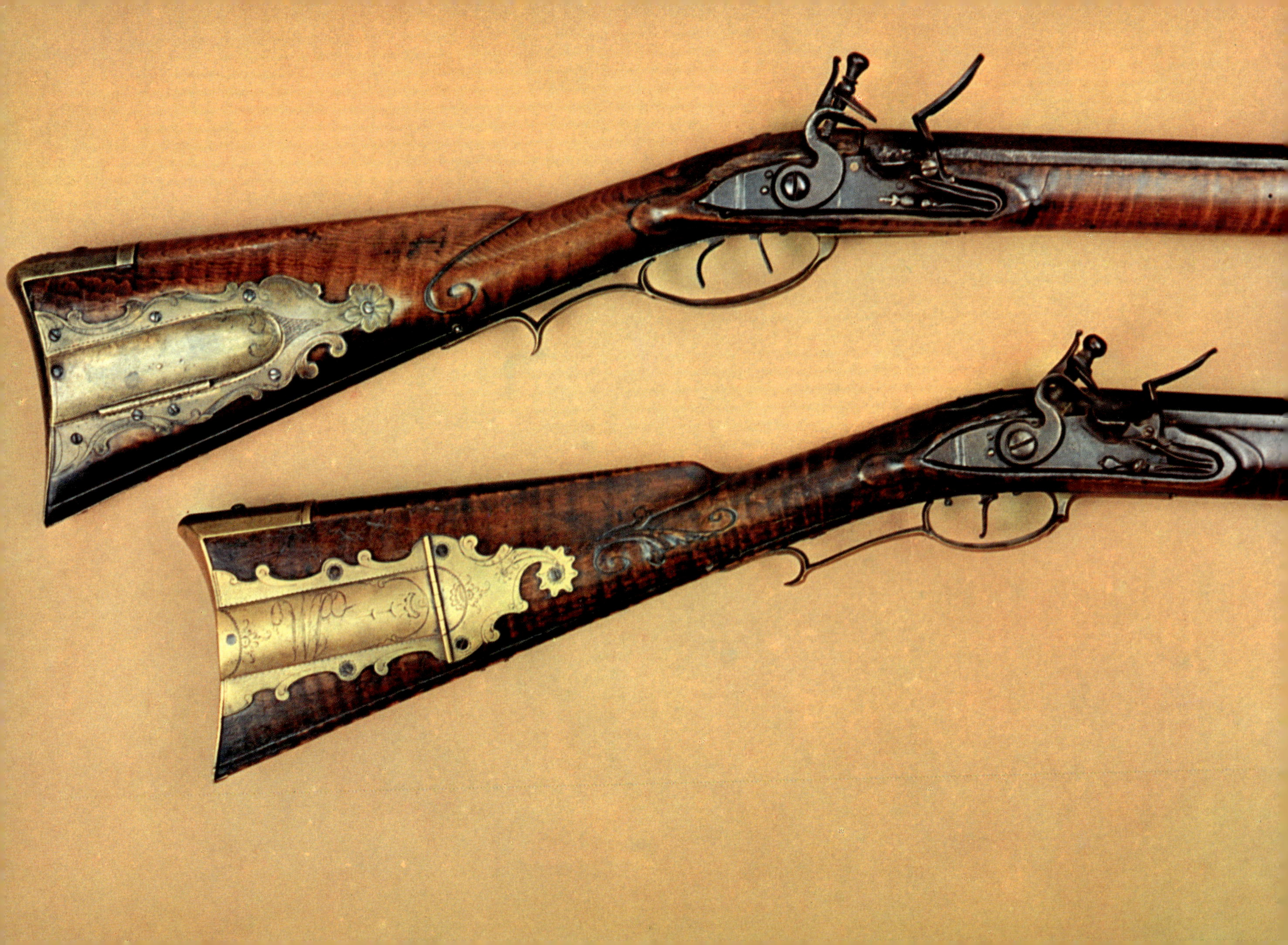

2. The Lancaster School

In all probability Lancaster was the original home of the Kentucky Rifle. The Lancaster Rifles are best recognized by the so-called daisy-headed patch box, the flower often integrated with engraved C-scrolls. Although occasionally found outside of this geographic area, it is still interrelated. Three screws generally secure the head of the daisy patch box to the stock.

Simple relief carved C-scrolls on the rear of the cheek piece are characteristic of this school as is the rather high straight comb profile of the stock and the thin wrist.

Left, top to bottom:

5. JACOB DICKERT (signed on barrel). Lancaster, Pa.
Much is known about Jacob Dickert. His gun barrels were the standard for accuracy in the Revolutionary War, and his daisy-headed patch box finials such as the one shown here were early examples if not the prototype of the Lancaster daisy. Dickert was born in Mainz in Germany in 1740, came to Berks County with his parents in 1748, moved with them to Lancaster in 1756, became a British subject in 1765, probably built rifles for the Continental Army (a later contract with the U.S. dated 1792 survives) and died in 1822. As he was eighty-two when he died, he had not been producing rifles for some years. Note the characteristic Lancaster stock shape and the fine engraving of the patch box frame. The bottom-hinged patch box, however, is more typical of Bucks County east of Reading, (see No. 16). Dickert was a prolific maker of fine rifles and rifle barrels and may have had apprentices helping him finish arms. Length overall 61¼ in., bbl. 45⅜ in.

Reverse of Nos. 5 & 6. Note the heavy cutout side plates.

6. J. FERREE (signed on barrel). Lancaster, Pa.
Ferree's rifle, shown at bottom left, exhibits two typical Lancaster characteristics, the daisy patch box finial and the straight lines of the buttstock when viewed in profile. The initials on the patch box are presumably those of the original owner. There were both a Jacob and a Joel Ferree who worked in Lancaster County. Joe Kindig thought that J. Ferree was probably Joel, who was listed as a gunsmith in the Leacock Township, Lancaster County, tax list of 1758. However Jacob may have made this rifle. He lived and worked in Strasburg Township, Lancaster County in the 1780s. Length overall 64½ in., bbl. 48⅛ in., .51 cal., rifled.

7. MELCHIOR FORDNEY (signed on barrel). Lancaster, Pa.

Melchior Fordney was a very good engraver. He worked in Lancaster at the end of the flintlock period well into the percussion era. He was apparently a conservative in his gunsmithing as most of his Kentuckys are equipped with flint locks. His private life was something else and that got him in trouble. He was living in god-fearing Lancaster with a lady to whom he was not married in 1846 when a religious nut named Haggerty hit him over the head for his sins and killed him. He had been working, according to the record, since 1811. His work is strong and imaginative. Note the punch work on the stripes above and below the patch box which has a horse-head finial characteristic of Littlestown instead of the typical Lancaster daisy. Length overall 61 in., bbl. 45⅛ in., .52 cal., smoothbore.

Detail of reverse of No. 7. Note the engraved side plate, the silver inlays back of the side plate and the checkering within the area defined by the overlapping rococo "C"s carved on the stock. There is an interesting repeat relationship between the silver oval and the larger oval checkered in the maple.

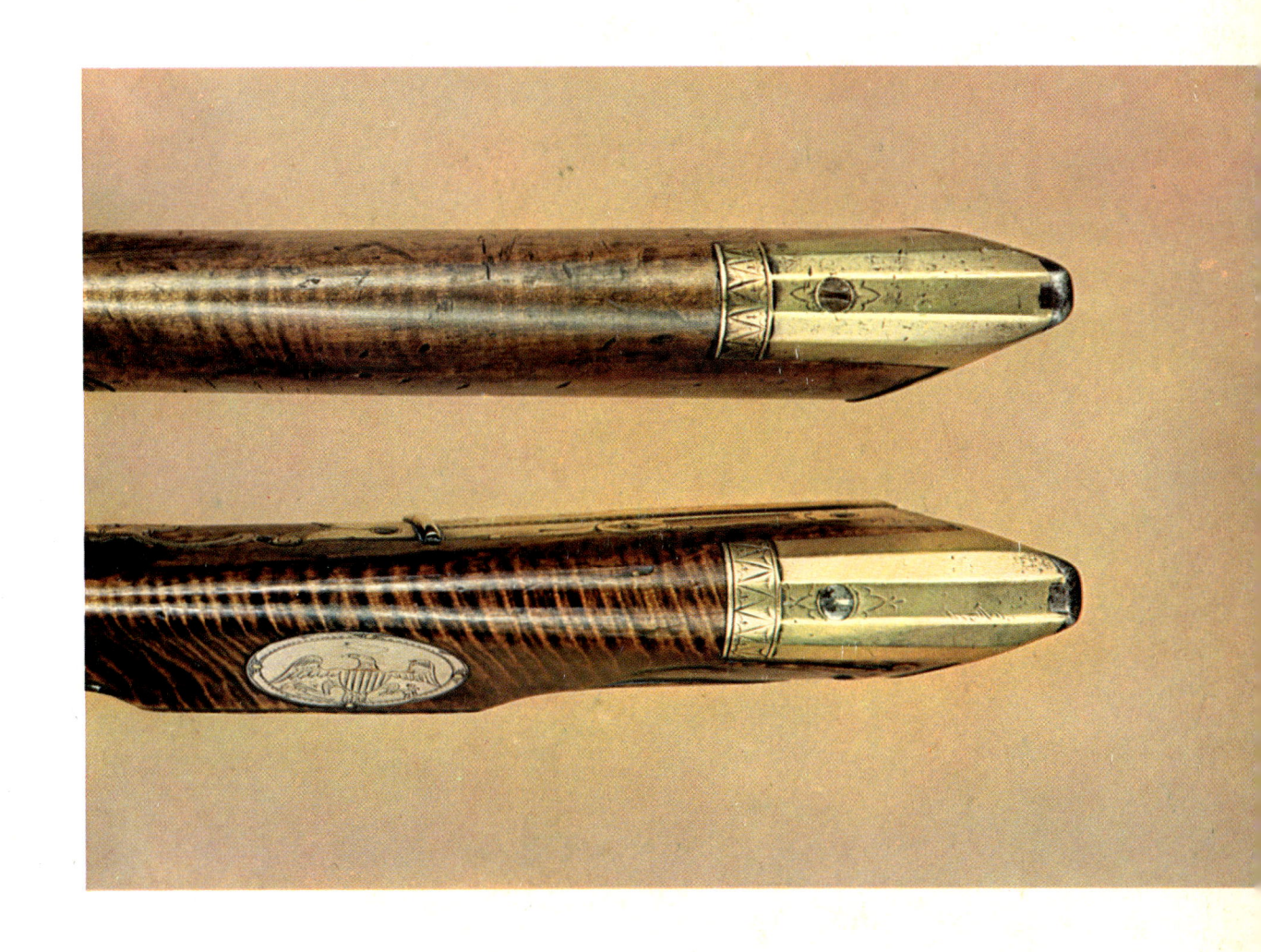

Detail of ornate under butt plate returns.

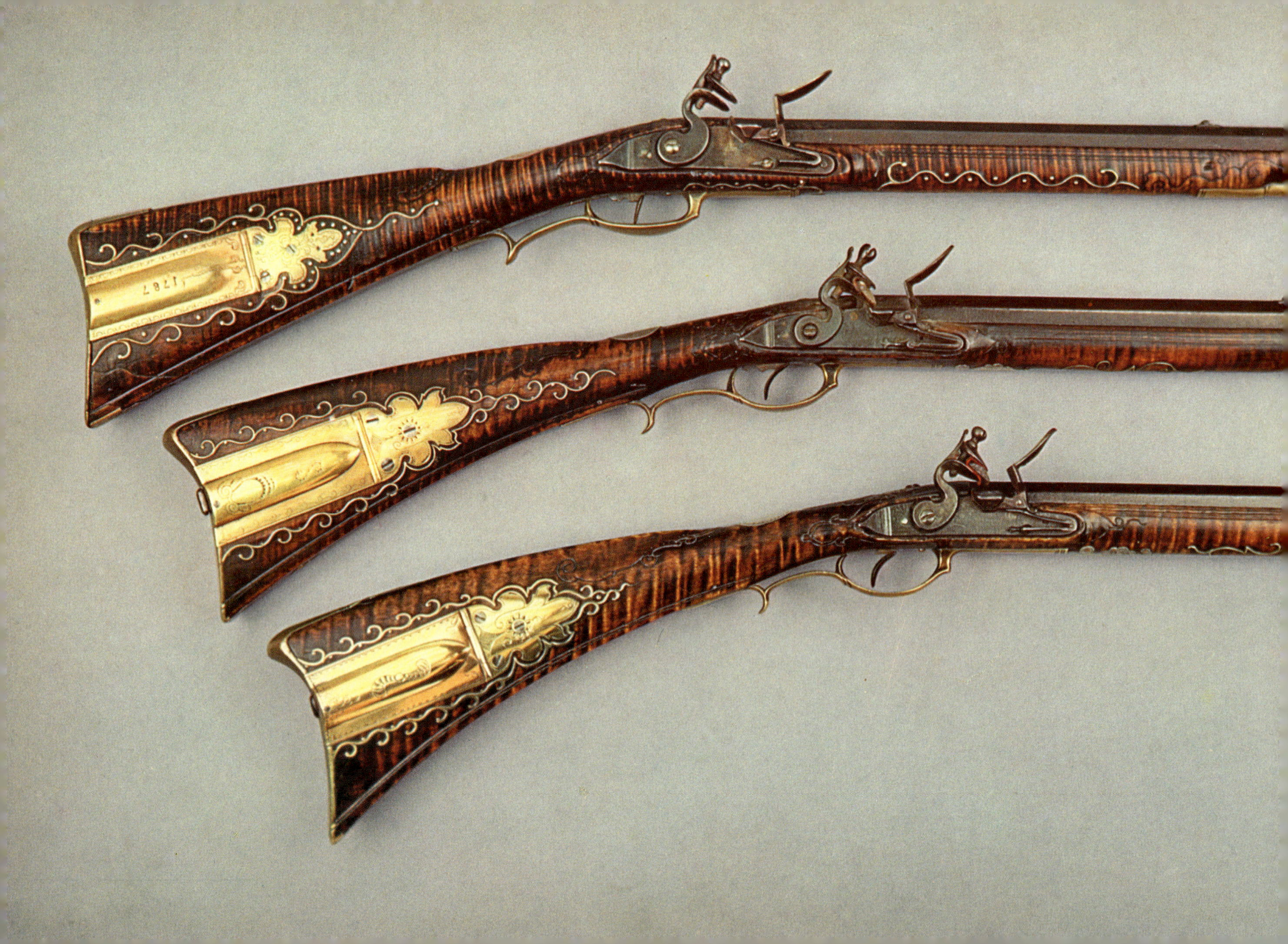
1787

3. The Bethlehem School

This school is best characterized by a fairly consistent occurrence of the so-called "Roman Nose" profile of the stock, produced by a slight convexity of the comb and concavity of the underside of the stock.

Early features, such as the thin, flat oval-shaped wrist, a simple two-part patch box and even sliding wooden patch boxes survived well into the 19th century.

In general, the engraving of the patch boxes was more frequently of inferior quality as was also the limited carving. The side plates often have an arrow-shaped terminal with the middle side plate screw set back.

The area is generally defined as North of the Schuylkill River and South of the Delaware River.

Left, top to bottom:

8. PETER NEIHART (signed on the barrel). Whitehall Township, Lehigh County, Pa.

This top piece, made by Peter Neihart does not have the strong Bethlehem "Roman Nose" which you see in the two guns below it. All three pieces share the grape tendril silver wire inlays and the dramatic flame-grained maple stocks. Neihart's gun is early as you can tell from the architecture as well as the inverted date "1787" on top of the cupped-out patch box. The cup or bulge is a design element derived from the older sliding wooden patch box covers. Except for a 1786 town tax record, Neihart is known only by his fine work. This is a good early example of a Bethlehem Kentucky. Length overall $58\frac{13}{16}$ in., bbl. $43\frac{1}{2}$ in., .52 cal., smoothbore.

9. HERMAN RUPP (signed and dated on barrel). Macungie Township, Lehigh County, Pa.

Six years after Peter Neihart made the top gun which is illustrated, Herman Rupp of Macungie made and signed this fine Bethlehem piece. It has more drop and the profile curves are greater, heightening the "Roman Nose" effect. Ahead of the trigger guard on this and the next Rupp gun are sheet silver cutouts representing an almond-eyed young lady with a pointy nightcap. These heads, sometimes called Indian heads, are often found on Bethlehem rifles. There is another one on No. 12, the Jacob Kuntz swivel breech. These are illustrated together a few pages further on. Still another is on a gun signed by a John Rupp illustrated in Joe Kindig's book and I have seen further examples in both the Herman Williams and the William Renwick collections. The Williams piece is unsigned and pre-Revolutionary with a wooden patch box cover and incised carving. The Renwick piece is signed on the barrel with a semi-legible "GM" or "WG" and there is some bird-scratch engraving on the patch box cover. The Renwick piece has twenty-one silver inlays and the typical Bethlehem "Roman Nose". The length of this gun: overall $63\frac{1}{2}$ in., bbl. $47\frac{1}{2}$ in., .61 cal., smoothbore.

10. HERMAN RUPP (signed and dated on the barrel). Macungie Township, Lehigh County, Pa.

This Rupp gun is dated 1809 which makes it sixteen years later. There isn't much change over the years in the two guns. There is slightly more profile curve and drop to the stock of the bottom gun, but the lower moulding line, the wire tendrils outlining the patch boxes and the under fore end inlays continue. The fine carving on these two Rupp guns is typical of the maker but not of the Bethlehem School. Length overall $58\frac{1}{2}$ in., bbl. $42\frac{1}{2}$ in., .47 cal., smoothbore.

Detail of No. 13. Patch box.

Overleaf, top to bottom:

11. PETER NEIHART (attributed). Whithall Township, Lehigh County, Pa.

Because of the "Roman Nose" stock shape this undated Neihart Kentucky is probably of a later date than the first Neihart rifle shown, (No. 8); this despite the reversion to the early type of wooden patch box which may have been done for economic reasons or because Neihart was short of brass or at the request of a conservative customer. Length overall 59½ in., bbl. 43¼ in., .50 cal., smoothbore.

12. JACOB KUNTZ (signed on the barrel and lock). Lehigh, Lehigh County, Pa.

Swivel breech Kentuckys are rare. Because of its extensive and elaborate carving and inlay work employing silver inserts and semi-precious stones, this wender rifle is rare to the point of being unique. Kuntz is obviously strongly influenced by the work and styles of European gunsmiths and stockmakers. His brace of rampant "Loew" or lion are supporting an American shield surmounted by an American single-headed eagle under a panoply of stars, but the whole left side of the gunstock with its jewel inset circled silver star on the cheek piece has a decidedly continental flavor. Kuntz is known to have worked in Lehigh, Pa. between 1799 and 1811 when he moved to Philadelphia. As the gun has an engraved silver insert in the lock plate which says "J. Kuntz in Lecha" and Lecha or Lechai was the name then for Lehigh the rifle was made before 1811. Note the elaborate tracery of the brass inlays around the patch box, the silver insert in the patch box cover and the inlay on the forestock behind the ramrod socket. Length overall 57 in., bbl. 40½ in. One barrel is .40 caliber, smoothbored, the other is .40 cal., rifled.

13. JOHN YOUNG (signed on the barrel and patch box lid). Easton, Pa.

This extra long gun made by engraver John Young is one of his early pieces. Other signed pieces are percussion and dated as late as the middle of the nineteenth century. His signed pieces are scarce. It is recorded that he was primarily an engraver who did work for other gunsmiths. The fine detail of the patch box shown opposite substantiates his engraving ability. Length overall 64⅛ in., bbl. 48⅜ in., .48 cal., smoothbore.

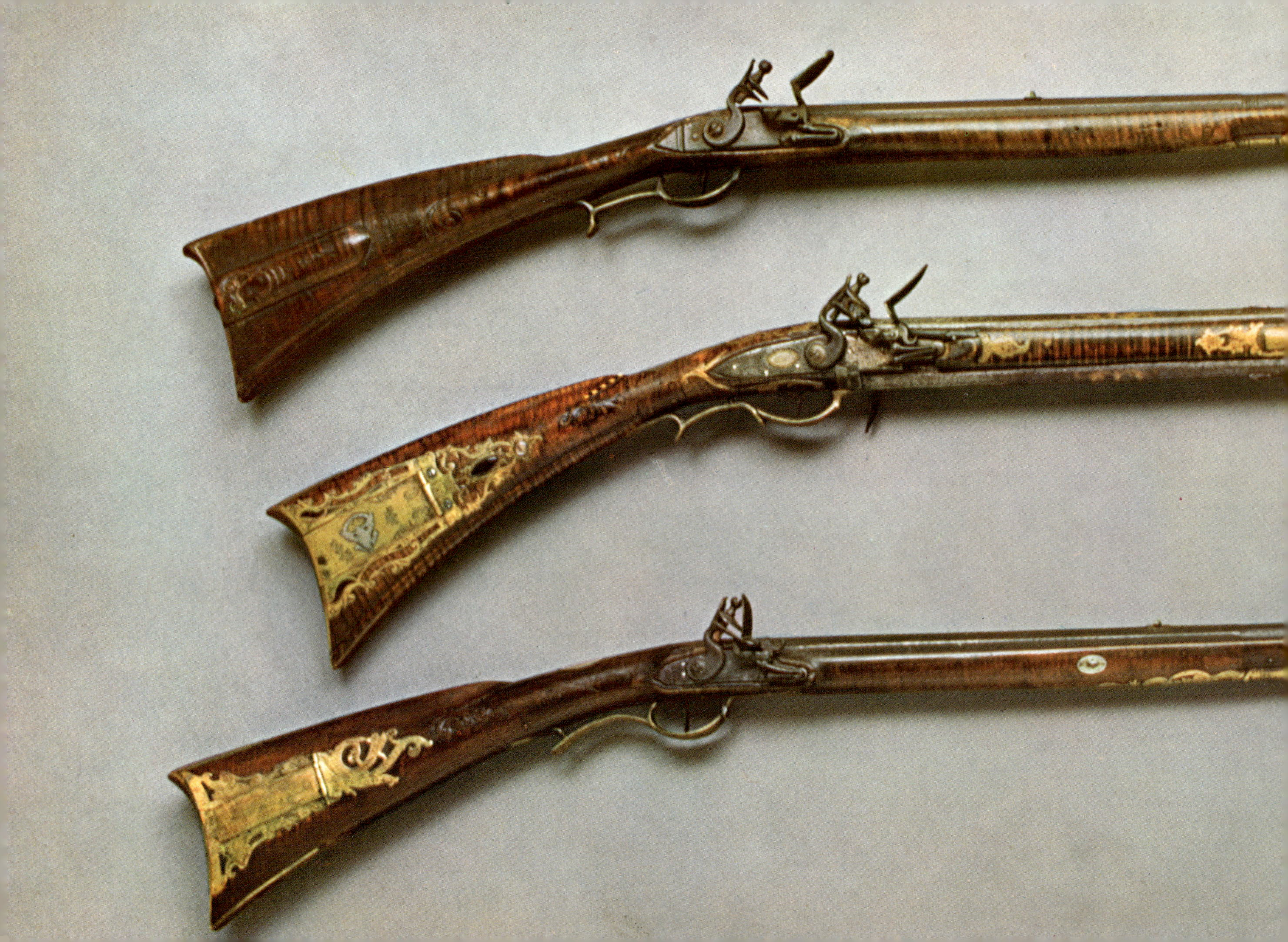

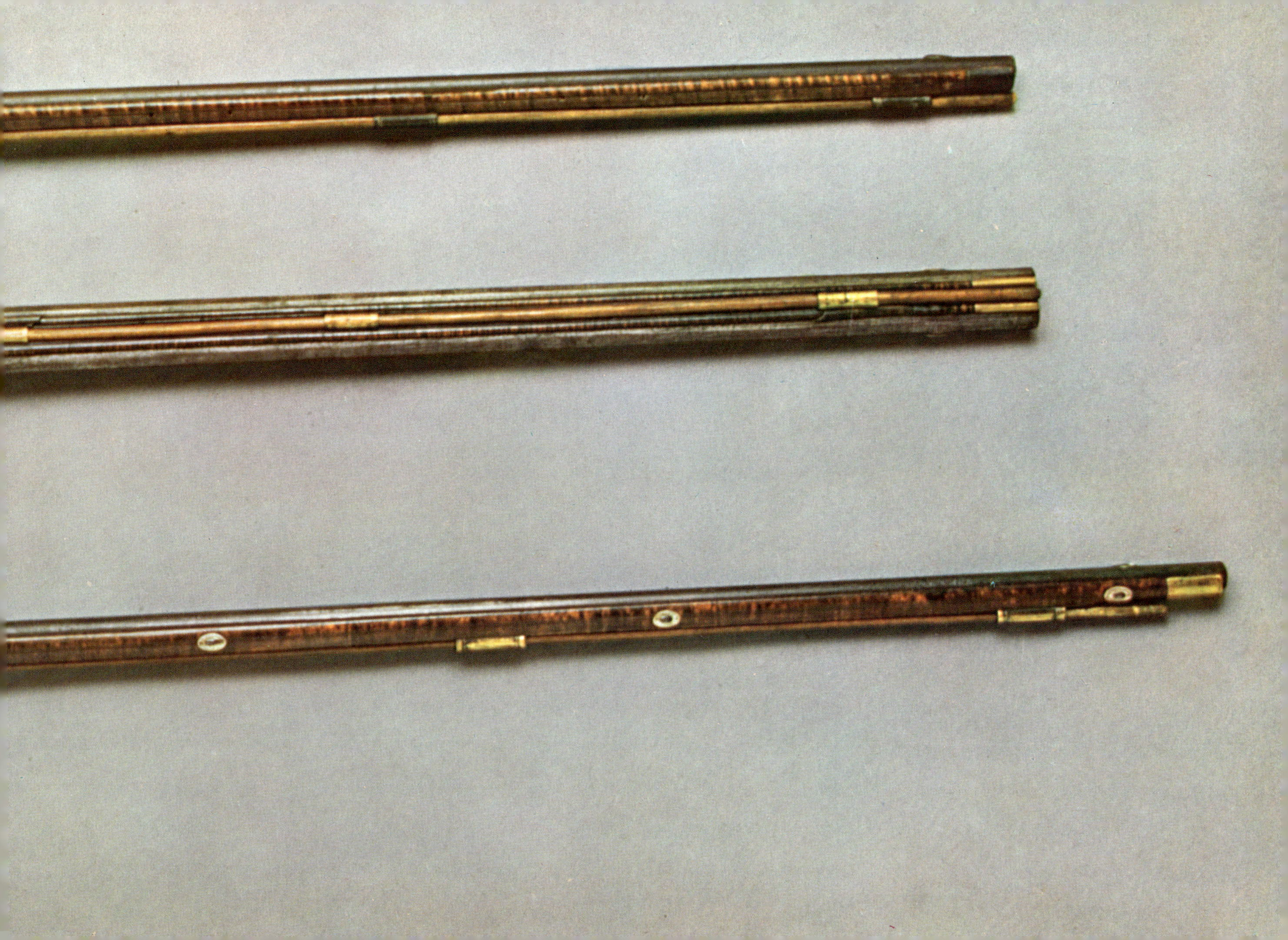

Detail of No. 9.

Detail of No. 10.

Detail of No. 12.

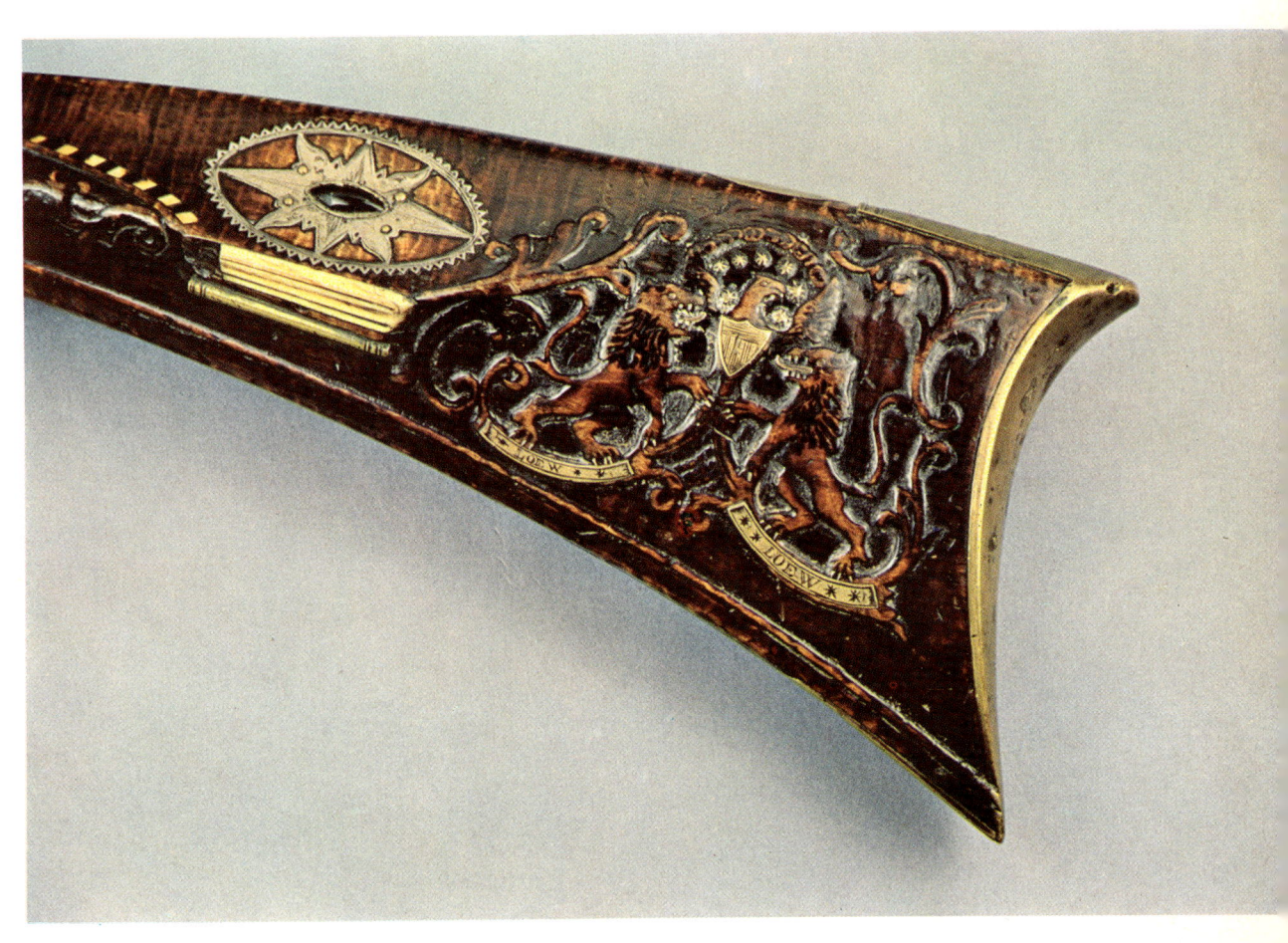

Detail of No. 12. Coat of arms.

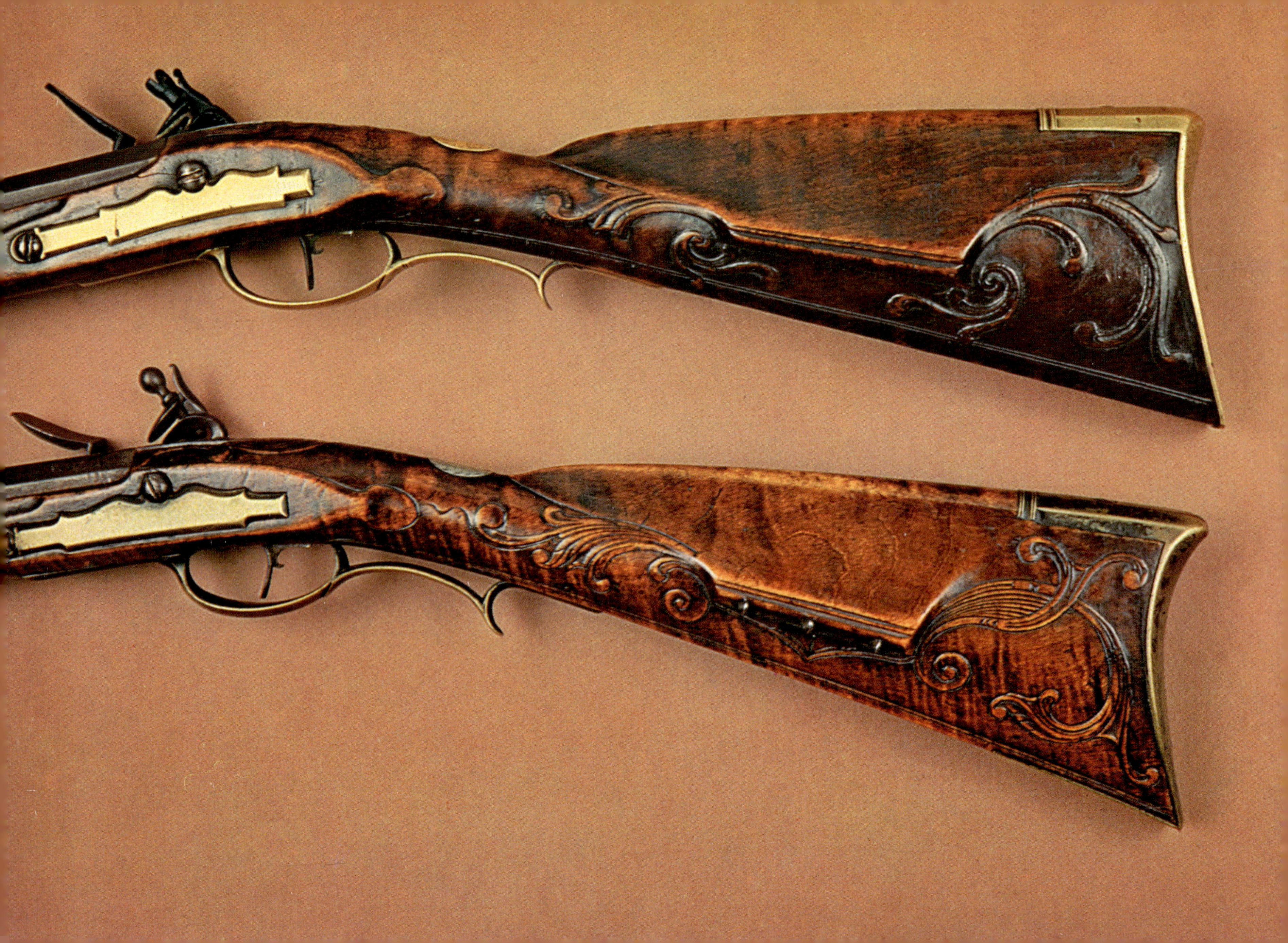

4. The Reading School

As the result of its geographical location, it was naturally influenced by both the Bethlehem and Lancaster Schools and was relatively contemporary to both. This is reflected in the stock architecture by the fairly high, straight comb and delicate wrist of Lancaster and in later examples by the "Roman Nose" of Bethlehem.

The patch boxes are generally more refined than in the Bethlehem school and the relief carving is well designed and executed.

Detail of cheek carving:

Left: 14. JOHN BONEWITZ (attributed). Womelsdorf, Western Berks County, Pa.
John Bonewitz is listed as a gunsmith in the local tax records in the years 1792 and 1800. Other records extend his known working period from 1779 to 1809. Bonewitz rarely signed his pieces, sometimes stamping them near the breech with a small die with the initials "I.B." which was a fine-furniture makers practice. Note the heavy beveled edges to the side plate and the flanges behind the forward screw which are characteristic Bonewitz touches. Also, the triggers are broad and flat with a little projecting hook to the rear. As Womelsdorf lies halfway between Reading and Lebanon it is not surprising that the shape and style reflect both schools. The relief carved "C" scrolls interrupting the bottom moulding are a Bonewitz innovation. Length overall 64⅜ in., bbl. 49¼ in., .52 cal., smoothbore.

Detail of No. 15. Patch box.

15. LEONARD REEDY (attributed). Dauphin County, Pa.
Few of Leonard Reedy's pieces are signed, but one that was led Samuel E. Dyke to look for a Kratz Town which was engraved on one barrel with Reedy's name on the other barrel of a flintlock over-and-under. Reedy was an inventive speller. It took Henry Kauffman to figure out that Kratz Town was Gratz, and sure enough Reedy's grave and that of his wife were discovered. A great-great-grandson of Reedy produced two of the gunmaker's account books. Reedy also spelled his name "Ready" and it appears on his tombstone as "Reedey". In his account books "rifle" becomes "ryfle" and rifle screws are "schrues" and "crues" and "meble blank" was a maple plank. As spelling came hard to Reedy his real signature is the fine design and carving which you see around the cheek piece of this gun. The design of the patch box illustrated above is not repeated on other Reedy guns. Reedy was born in 1774 and worked from 1792 until his death in 1837. He averaged about three guns a year. Length overall 58¼ in., bbl. 42¼ in., .48 cal., smoothbore.

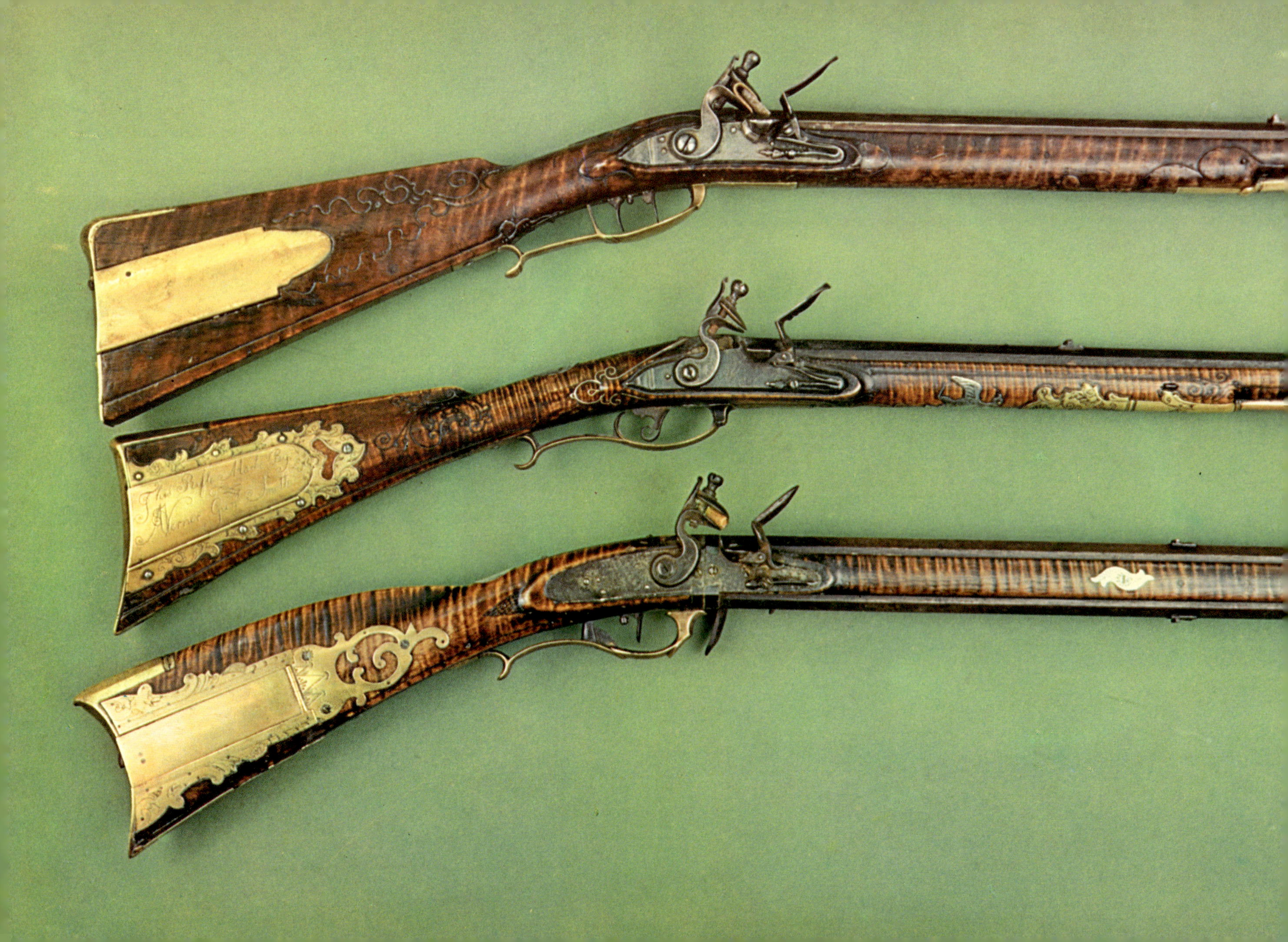

5. *The Associated Bethlehem School*

Under the influence of the Bethlehem school, this area east of Reading produced rifles with quality carving and engraving of a high order. Occasionally, patch boxes appear of under-hinged form, rarely seen outside of this area. In general, the stock profile combines the Lancaster high straight comb with the "Roman Nose" of the Bethlehem school and a bird or lion motif sometimes appears in the carving.

This school includes Kutztown, Easton, and Quakertown.

Left, top to bottom:

16. UNKNOWN. Attributed to the region northeast of Lancaster.
This rifle has a pre-Revolutionary shape and simplicity and sturdiness despite its brass patch box and double set triggers. The plain patch box hinges at the bottom as does the patch box on the gun below and the Dickert gun (No. 5). This suggests that the arm was made somewhere east of Reading or in Bucks County. Note the flat angularity of the trigger guard and the sparse but effective incised decoration. Length overall 61⅞ in., bbl. 45⅝ in., .48 cal., rifled.

17. A. VERNER (signed on patch box lid). Bucks County, Pa.
There was an Andrew Verner in Bucks County, Pa., listed in the U.S. census made in 1790. Joe Kindig thought that this must have been the "A. Verner Gun Smith". The bottom-hinged patch box is a Bucks County feature. Also, according to Kindig's deduction, the silver double-headed eagle inlaid under the forestock is Imperial German and the rifle is pre-Revolutionary. After the Revolution, the eagle would have had a single head and a shield on his breast. See the details of the patch box and the sheet silver eagle on the following pages and note the fancy back-curved trigger. Length overall 62 5/16 in., bbl. 46½ in., .47 cal., smoothbore.

18. ADAM ANGSTADT (signed on the barrel with initials "A.A."). Kutztown, Pa.
Except for the fact that this is a swivel breech or wender, it is representative of the rifles made in the Kutztown school and by the Angstadt family. The Angstadts were such a large family of gunsmiths (working in the period circa 1800-1810) that they practically constituted their own school. The "Roman Nose" is both Angstadt and Bethlehem. Length overall 56½ in., bbl. 40⅜ in., both barrels .38 cal., rifled.

Detail of patch box of No. 17.

Detail of fore end and sheet metal decoration of No. 17.

Detail of cheek piece carving of No. 16 & No. 17.

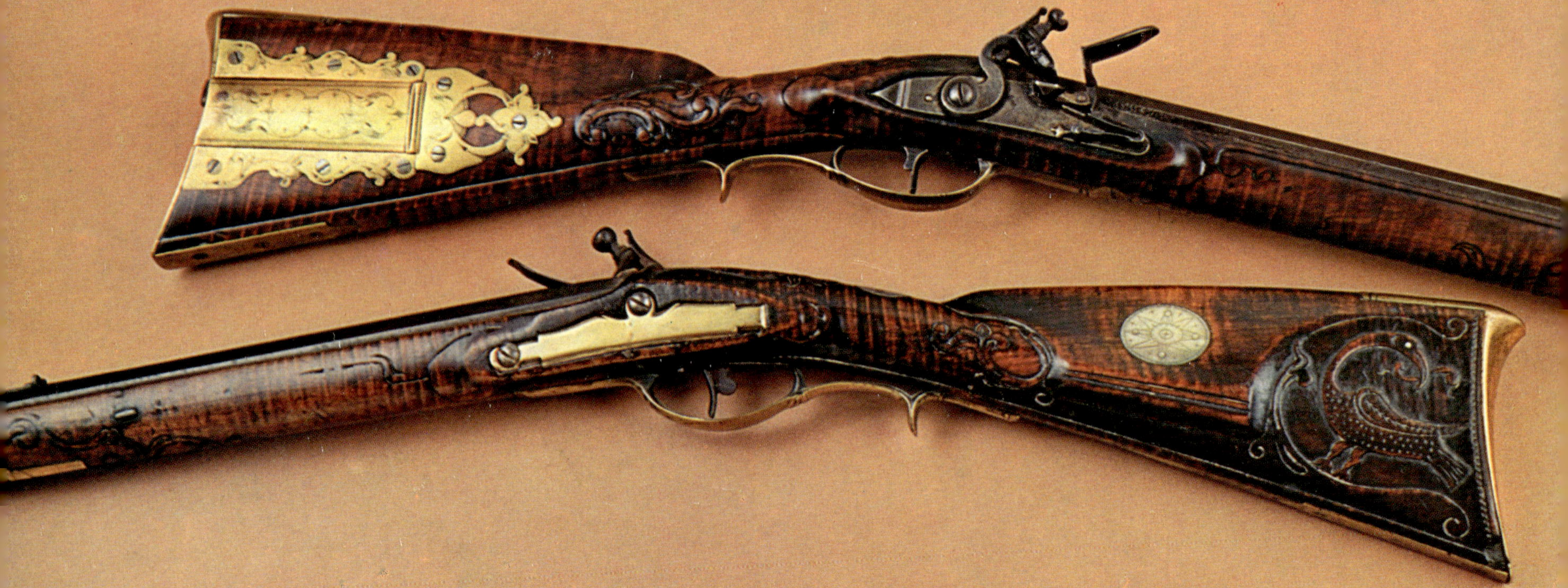

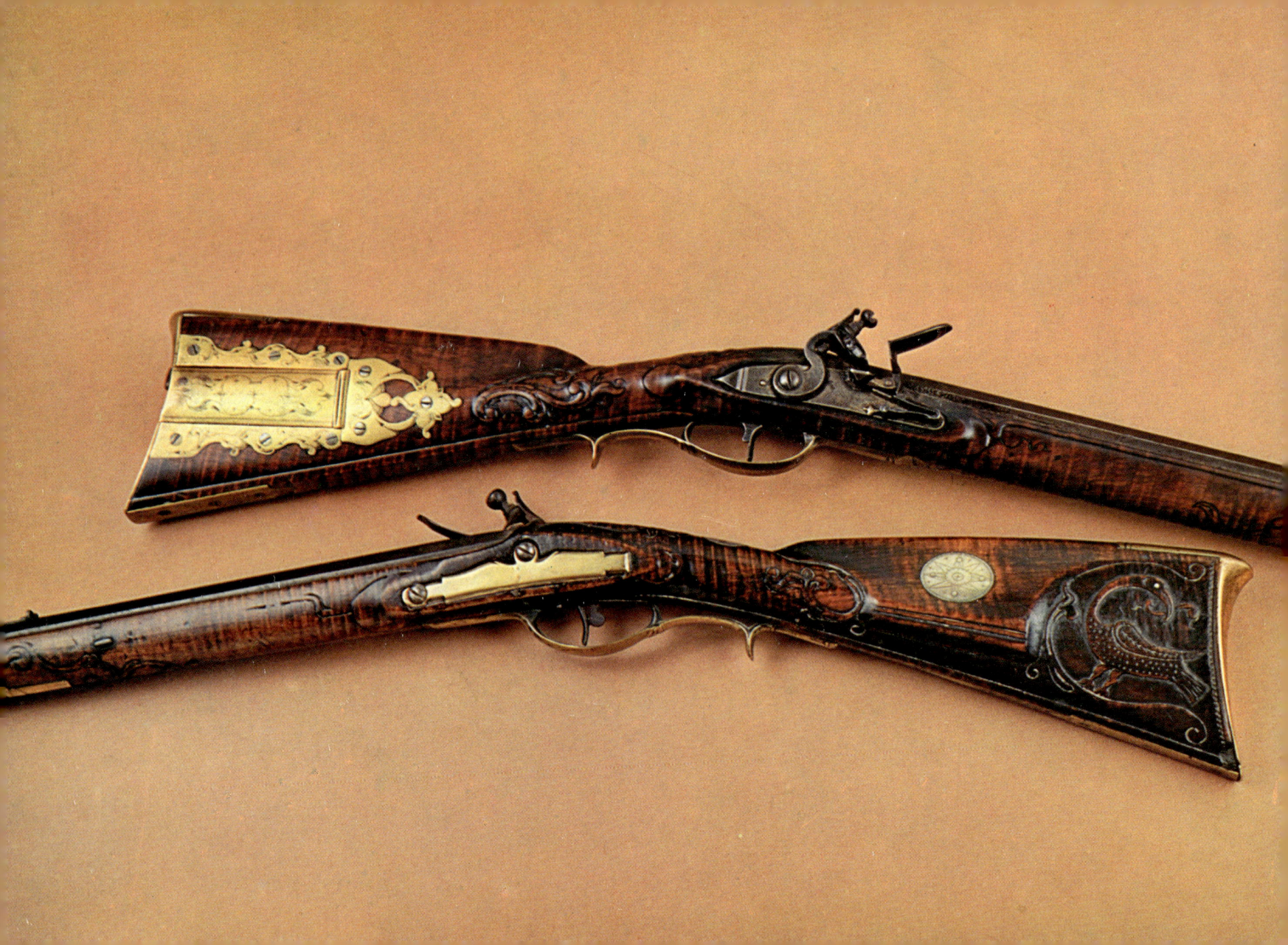

6. The Lebanon School

Guns of this school, centered around the town of Lebanon, exhibit particularly beautifully designed patch boxes with a restrained amount of rather shallow engraving and a great variety of patch box heads.

The long wrist and the high comb combine to produce a handsome stock profile which was ornamented with a great variety of well-designed and finely executed high relief carving ranging from sophisticated rococo to folk art subjects. The cheek pieces are sometimes accented with a heavy three ribbed moulding. Unlike some of the early schools, a high percentage of these rifles are signed.

Some of the finest of the early rifles are to be found in this school. The examples selected permit a comparison of the sophisticated work of Beck with the folk art of Beyer.

Left, top to bottom:

19. JOHN PHILIP BECK (signed with initials on the thumb piece). Lebanon, Pa.

The classic work of J. P. Beck has already been illustrated in the pre-Revolutionary chapter. Although this rifle has a single-headed eagle on the cheek piece instead of the double eagle which appears on one of his earlier pieces, master gunsmith Beck has retained the formal rococo style and has executed his carving with expertise in high relief. Beck was only two years old when he arrived in America from Rotterdam on the ship *Richard and Mary*, but he acquired a knowledge of European styling, possibly from his father. This gun com-

Reverse sides of Nos. 19 & 20.

pares favorably in workmanship with flintlock schuetzen rifles being made in Germany in the middle of the eighteenth century. The underside of the barrel of this rifle is engraved with the letter I N R I which stand for Iesus Nazarenus Rex Iudaeorum, "Jesus of Nazareth, King of the Jews." Length overall $57\frac{3}{16}$ in., bbl. 42 in., .47 cal., rifled.

20. NICHOLAS BEYER (signed on the barrel). Lebanon, Pa.

Nicholas Beyer was one of John Beck's best pupils. He learned the craft and skills from the master gunsmith but he used these techniques to represent the themes of Pennsylvania folk art rather than the more formal rococo designs. Beyer frequently used pierced bird-shaped patch box finials such as the one shown. The evil-looking bird carved in the buttstock back of the cheek is imaginative as well as folk art. Length overall $62\frac{1}{8}$ in., bbl. 47 in., .49 cal., smoothbore.

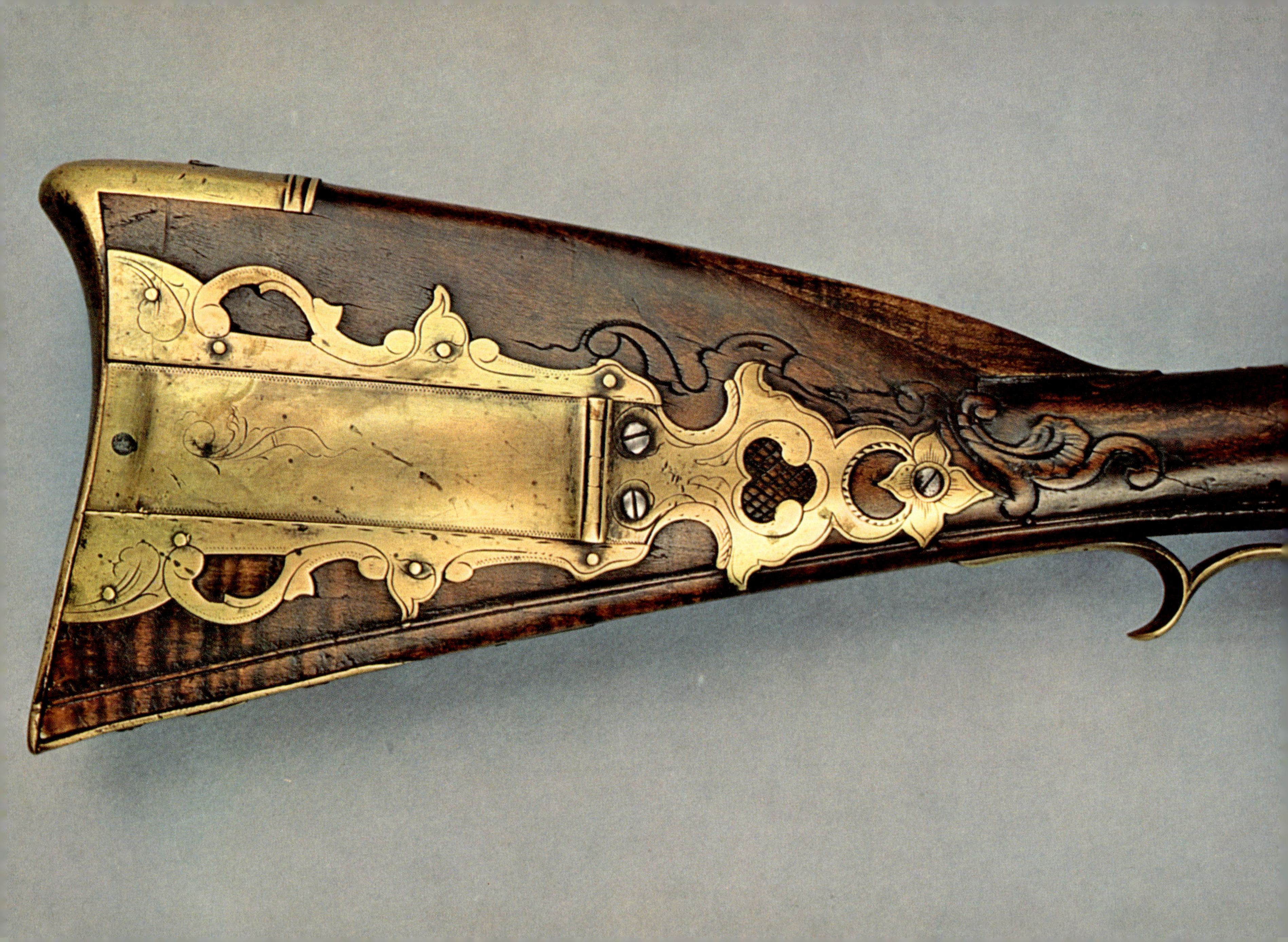

7. *The Dauphin School*

Characteristics of the Dauphin School are not as well defined as in some of the others but it may be said that architecturally they produced a relatively graceful long rifle with a high straight comb, a long wrist and the bottom edge of the stock frequently relieved with a lower butt moulding.

The typically slightly off-center patch box mounted at an angle is generally well-designed and pierced with a 3 or 4 petal flower head. Brass and silver wire inlay, infrequently found in Kentucky rifles, occurs in the work of gunsmiths of this school.

Left: Patch box of No. 21. PETER BERRY (signed). Dauphin, Pa. Peter Berry was an exceptionally fine maker of long slender guns with beautiful patch boxes and unusually fine carving. This is a first-rate example of his work as well as a typical example of the best of the Dauphin school. Note the off-center patch box interrupting the lower moulding with its four-petal flower-head finial. Peter Berry probably worked in Heidelberg Township, Dauphin County between 1780 and his death in 1795.

Detail of lower butt moulding of No. 21.

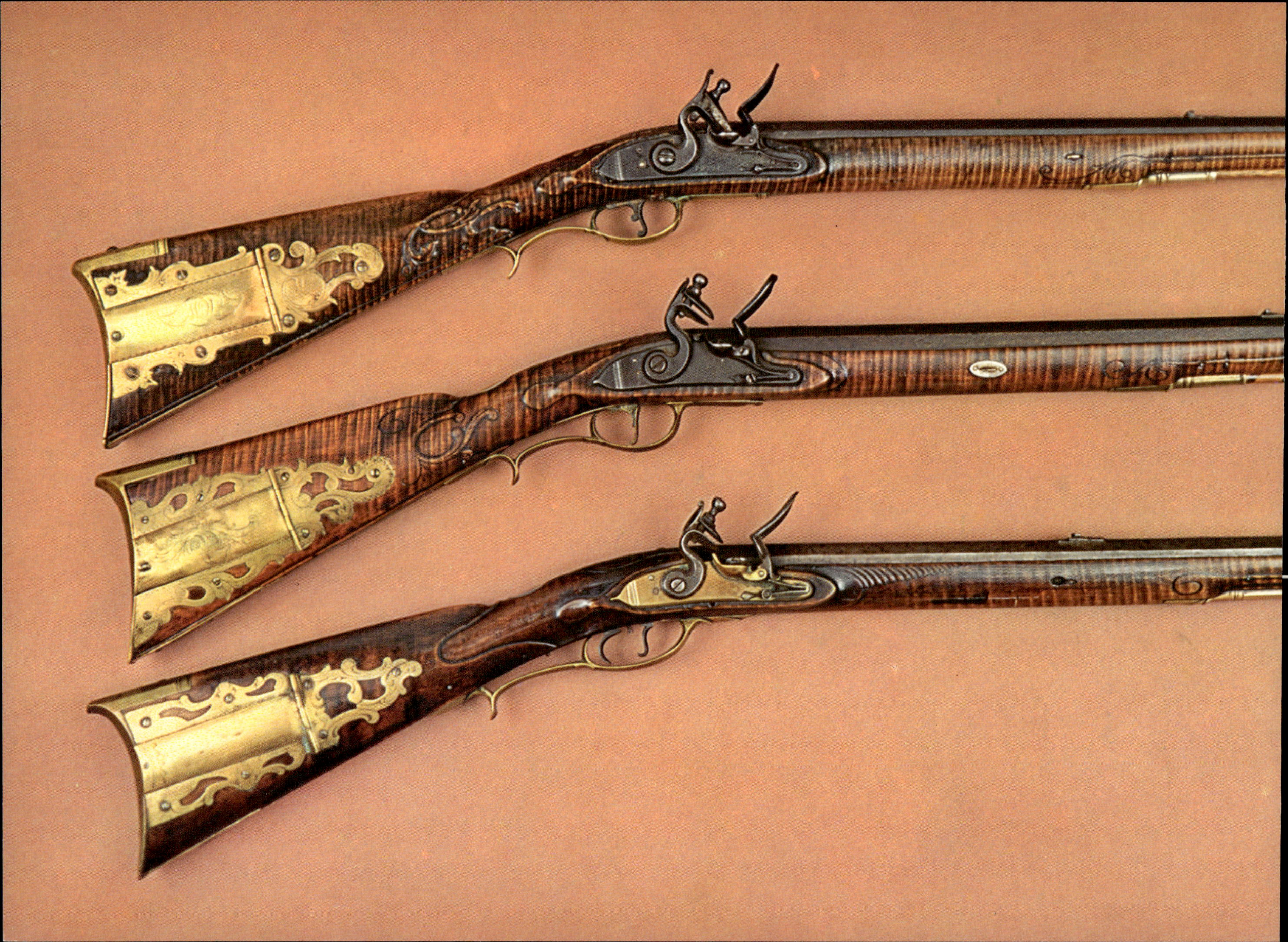

8. The York School

This school reflects more of a really great center of gunsmithing than it does the exchange, or sharing of artistic ideas typical within most schools.

The keen competition among gunsmiths as a result of the demands for rifles during the Revolution when York was a temporary capital produced a degree of artistic excellence seldom exceeded in other schools.

The York guns exhibit an architecture with a Lancaster flavor—not at all surprising when you consider the proximity of their older eastern neighbor.

York gunsmiths on the whole designed and engraved a remarkable variety of unusually beautiful patch boxes. Their carving too, often in high relief, is composed largely of artistically integrated rococo C-scrolls and varies notably from gun to gun. A silver cheek piece and thumb plate are usually the only silver inlays to adorn York Kentuckys. The only detail used extensively by York gunsmiths and almost never by any other is the tapered rear ramrod pipe.

Left, top to bottom:

22. HENRY PICKEL (signed "H. Pickel" on the barrel and "Pickel" on the lock). York, Pa.

Pickel's gun is shown top left here and the cheek side of the stock two pages later. The classic rococo carving is worthy of the finest Philadelphia Chippendale furniture of the last two decades of the eighteenth century. The patch box finial and the engraving of the side plates and finial are typical of York. Length overall 59¼ in., bbl. 43 3/16 in., smoothbore.

23. FREDERICK ZORGER (signed on the barrel F. Zorger). York, Pa.

Frederick Zorger's tombstone, six miles north of York, shows that he was born in December 1734 and died May 28, 1815. He was a gunsmith of record during the Revolutionary War. His gun, the middle one illustrated here, is a perfect example of York workmanship and design, at the end of the eighteenth century. A pair of rococo "C" scrolls form the base of the patch box finial on Zorger's rifle and the one below it. Length overall 57⅞ in., bbl. 42½ in., rifled.

24. ADAM ERNST (signed on barrel A. Ernst). York, Pa.

Adam Ernst worked in Adams County and York County between 1805 and the time he died in 1857 at the age of seventy-six. He seems to have learned the gunsmithing trade from George Eister of York. The use of brass for the lock plate is unusual. It may have been made in York by Ernst or one of his apprentices. The rifle with its set trigger mechanism was probably made at the end of the flintlock period, between 1810 and 1820. Length overall 59 in., bbl. 43⅛ in., rifled.

Left: Detail of sight of No. 25. GEORGE EISTER (attributed). York, Pa.

This target rifle by George Eister is unusual in employing such fine workmanship on what would normally be a plain piece. The tubular tin sun shade used in target shooting contrasts with the shaping, carving and finish of the stock. Eister's work is similar to Zorger's in some of the detail and his treatment of rococo decoration has the distinct flavor of the York school which is also evident in the work of other York masters including Andrew Kopp, Frederick Sell, John Armstrong, Samuel Grove and Adam Ernst. This target gun is 59¾ inches long with a 43 7/16 inch barrel.

Right: Carving of No. 22, No. 24 and rifle No. 26. GEORGE SCHREYER (signed G. Schreyer on the barrel). Hanover, Pa.

George Schreyer (Schroyer, Scheyer, Schryer, Shroyer and Shryer are some of the variants) was a great Pennsylvania gunsmith who worked his way west from Reading and settled in Hanover in York County the year before the Revolution. He was probably descended from a large family of Austrian and South German gunsmiths working between 1664 and 1745 who spelled their name Scherer or Scheurer. Cf. Kindig p. 375. The Schreyer rifle has a typically high comb and the silver is limited to the oval cheek piece and thumb plate. There is a flower design carved in the stock behind the barrel tang which Schreyer uses often enough to become an identification of his pieces. Length overall 60¼ in., bbl. 44⅜ in., rifled.

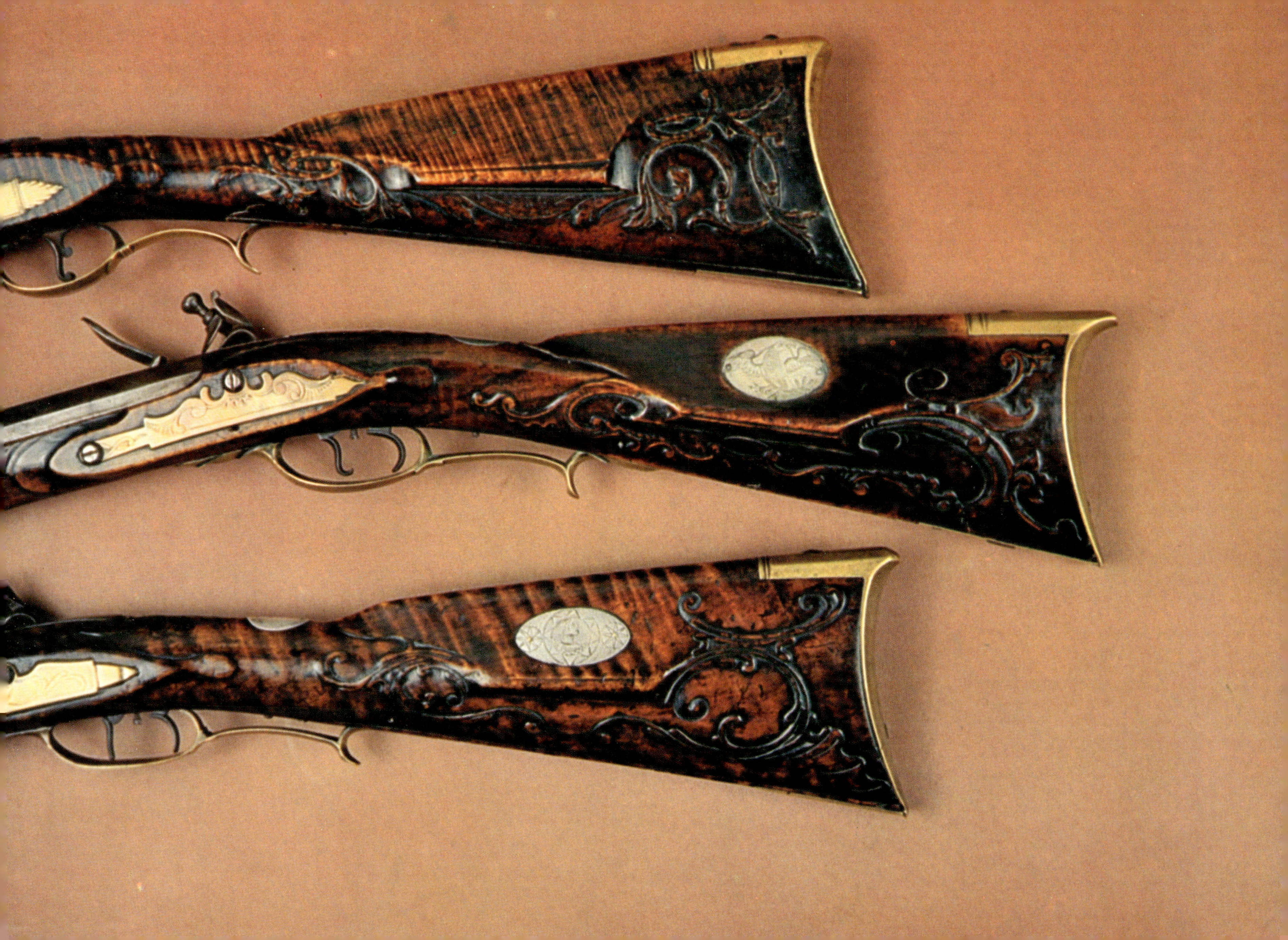

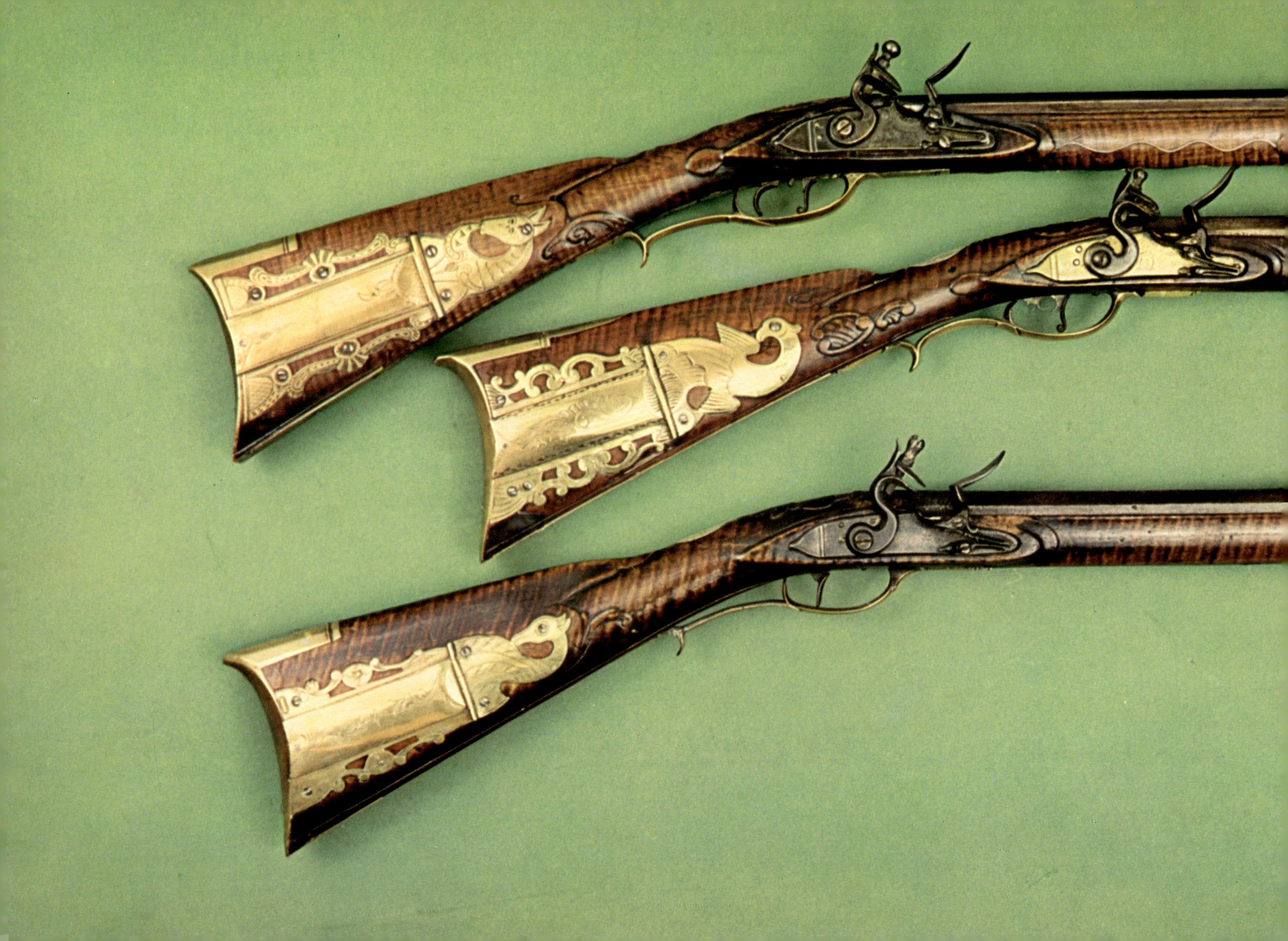

9. The Littlestown School

This school is comprised of a relatively small, though highly artistic and prolific group of gunsmiths. Kentuckys produced here from before the Revolution until after 1825 exhibit a variety and richness of engraved and carved detail seldom equaled in other schools.

Their patch boxes are typically large, frequently pierced and sometimes display bird, animal or human figures in the head. Typically, the patch boxes and other metal mounts are generously ornamented with well-designed and skillfully wrought C-scroll engraving.

Although carving on the straight, high combed stocks of this area varies notably from gun to gun, it is characteristically rich in rococo C-scroll foliation executed in high relief and frequently designed to be compatible with adjacent engraved detail.

Left, top to bottom:

27. JOHN SHRIVER (signed on the barrel and dated below the cheek piece). Adams County, Pa.

John Shriver was proud to be living in the newly created Adams County which had been created out of the western part of York County so he commemorated the event by engraving the county name on a brass plate which he inlaid on the top flat of the barrel of this piece. Another brass barrel inlay has his name, "Jno. Shriver" and a third below the cheek piece has the date "May 15, 1801". The horse- or mule-headed patch box finial could not be more typical of the school. The silver wire inlay in the fore end, the silver eagle with wings spread on the cheek, the engraving on the side plate and patch box frame and on the inlay under the cheek piece as well as the cross-hatched chevrons on the fore end cap rate John Shriver among the foremost gunsmiths in Pennsylvania. Length overall 58⅛ in., bbl. 42 3/16 in., .48 cal., rifled.

28. FREDERICK SELL (signed on the barrel). Littlestown, Pa.

Frederick Sell was one of the Kentucky rifle master gunsmiths. He started to work as a freeman gunsmith in downtown York in 1807, moved to Littlestown in 1816 with a wife. There he devoted himself full time to gun making. He died in 1869. The Pegasus patch box finial, the relief carving on the throat, the homemade brass lock plate with the initials "F.S.", the shaped and pierced trigger and the chevron grooved fore end cap make this Sell rifle outstanding. Length overall 59 9/16 in., bbl. 43 11/16 in., .41 cal., rifled.

29. JACOB SELL, THE YOUNGER (signed on top of the barrel in script). Littlestown, Pa.

Jacob Sell the Younger was the brother of Frederick Sell. He was born in 1780 and died in 1855. He learned gunsmithing from his father whom he exceeded both as a carver and as an engraver. His work is more sensitive than that of his brother Frederick. Kindig says: "He understood the proportion and curve of the "C" scroll and he utilized them to the best advantage." Length overall 60⅞ in., bbl. 45 5/16 in., .46 cal., rifled.

Left, above: Detail of chevron–cross-hatched fore end cap of Nos. 27 & 28.

Left, below: Detail of No. 28. Homemade lock plate and pierced trigger.

Right: Detail of reverse of Nos. 27, 28, & 29.

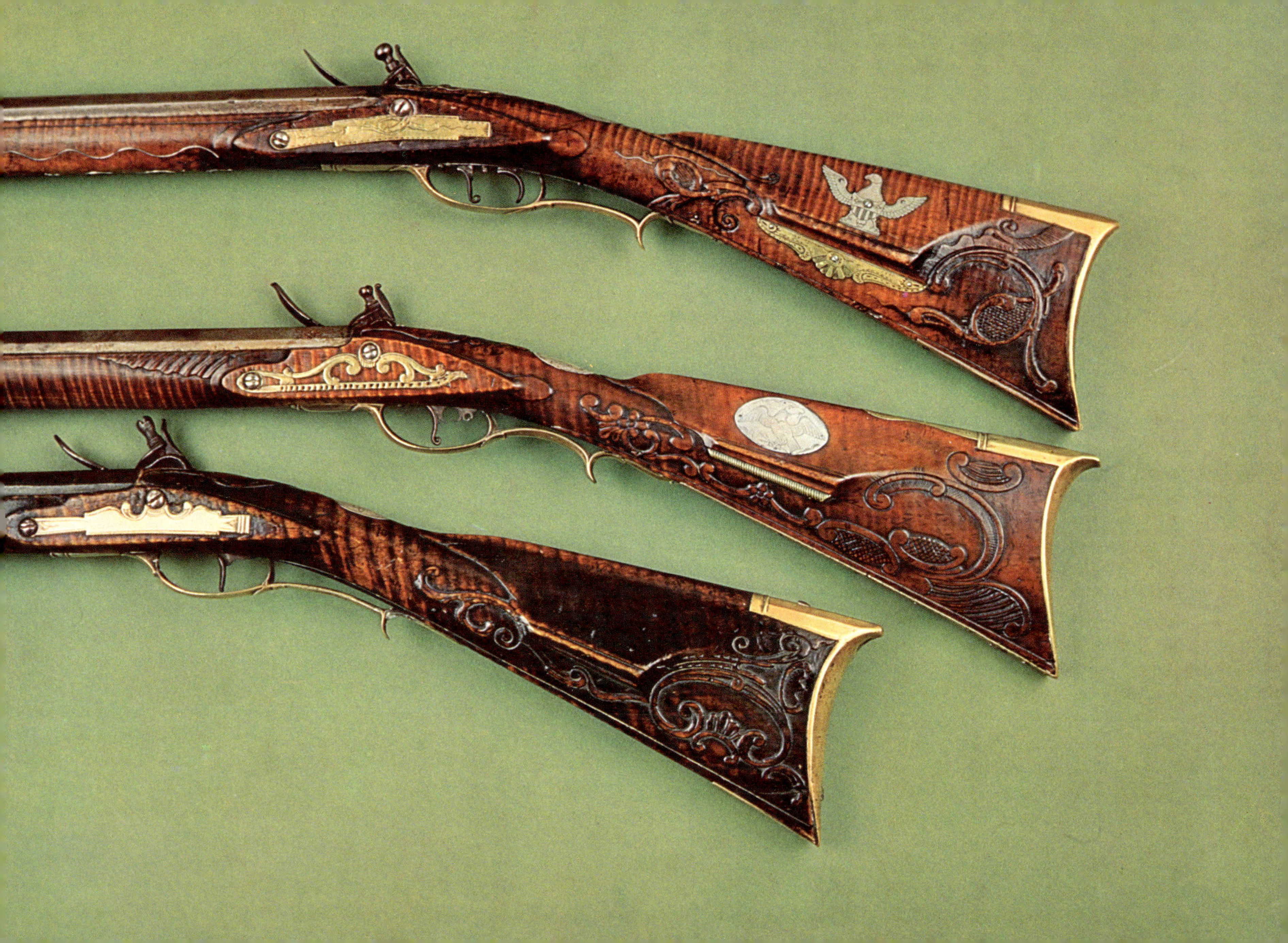

Above: Detail of No. 27. Barrel plate "Adams County".

Left, above: Detail of No. 27. Barrel plate "J^{no.} Shriver".

Left, below: Detail of No. 28. Barrel plate "Frederick Sell".

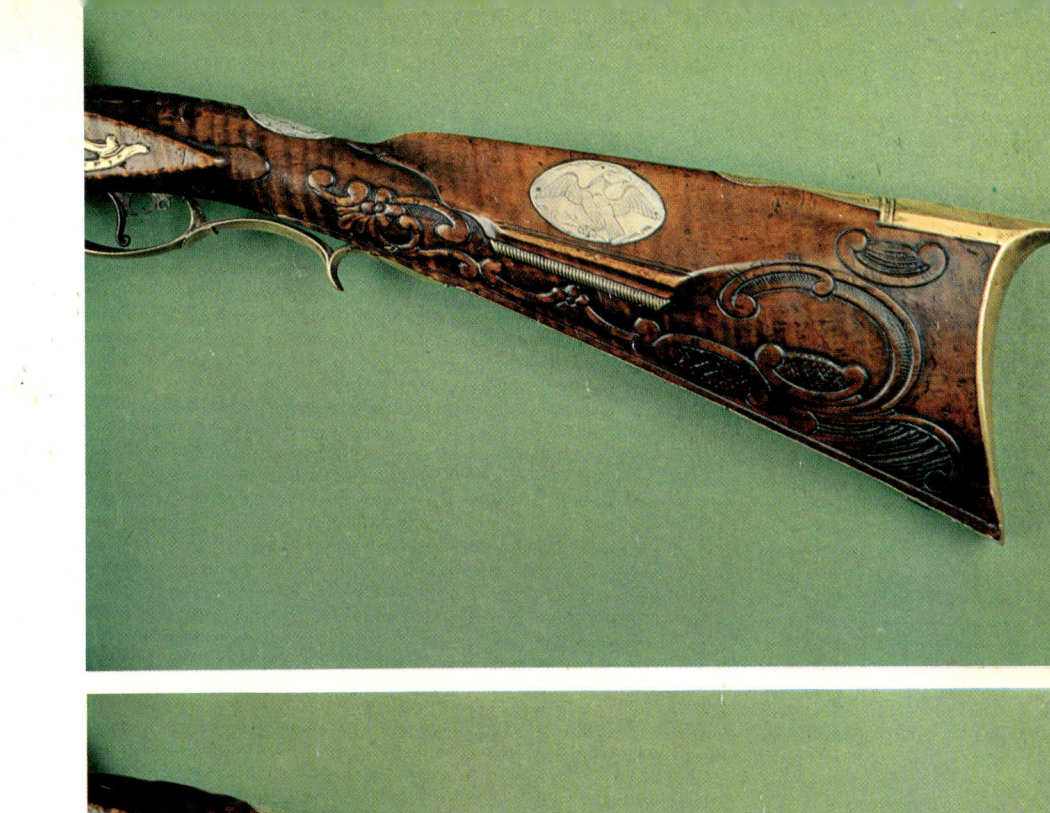

Detail of No. 28. Cheek piece.

Detail of No. 29. Cheek piece.

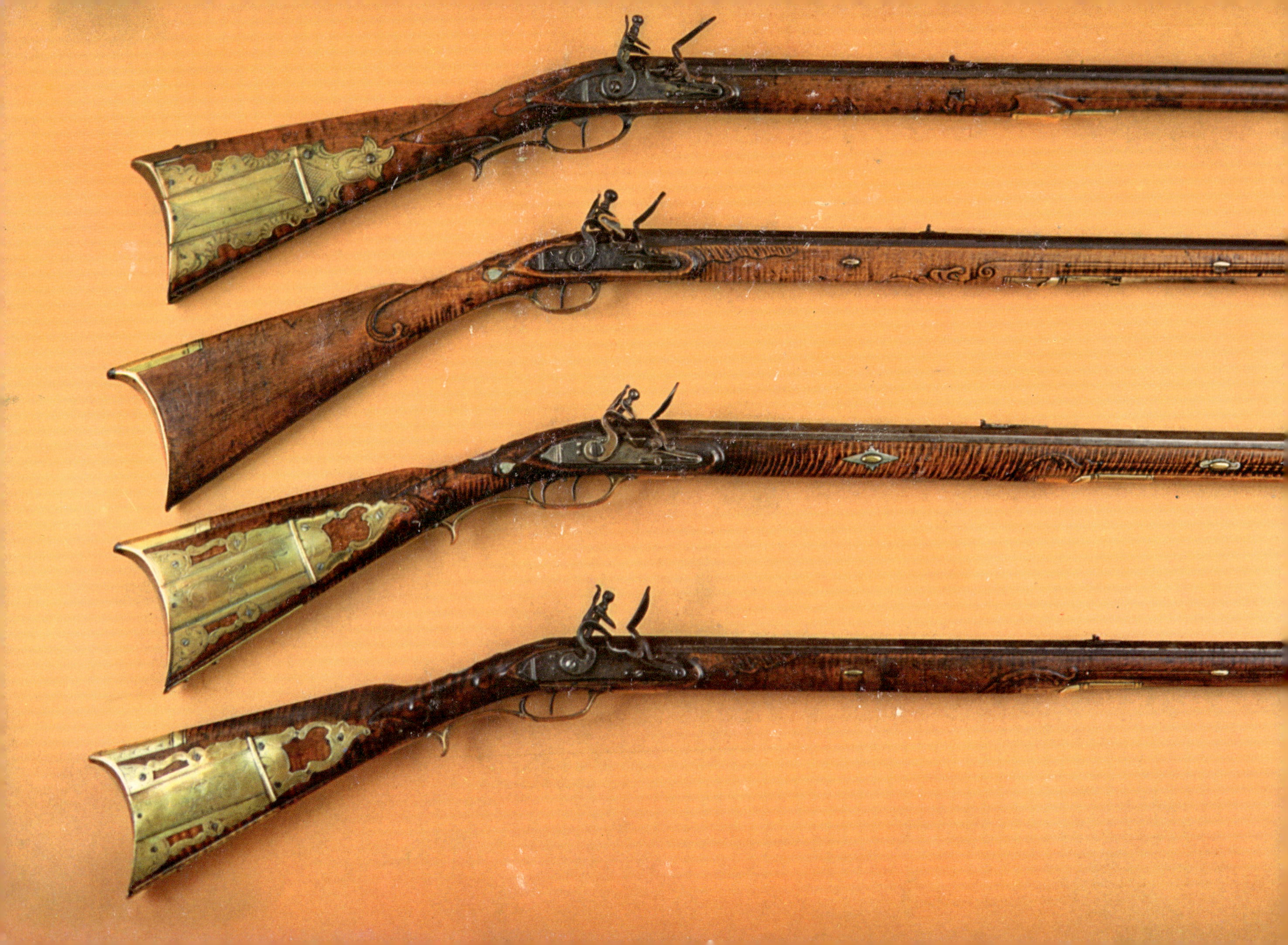

10. The Emmitsburg School

Within certain Schools of gunsmithing, the influences of various master gunsmiths on their journeyman and apprentice, as well as on other gunsmiths, is much stronger and more significant than in other schools. This is particularly true of the Emmitsburg school.

George Schreyer was a generation older than John Armstrong and worked in nearby Hanover; five details used by Schreyer are reflected in Armstrong's work. These include the cameo cutting of the stock to show a separation of the throat from the butt, Schreyer's characteristic moulding, the engraving on the butt cap return, the gadroon effect in the forestock just ahead of the lock, and Schreyer's individual buttstock shape.

A fine example of Armstrong's early period is illustrated here in a flintlock. It is followed by an example of his middle period made in the 1820's but it shows no lowering of his standards. Another rare work of his is to be seen in a fowling piece. A fully developed example of Armstrong's apprentice, Nathaniel Rowe, is shown, demonstrating his adaptation of Armstrong's style. These Kentucky rifles illustrate the strong influence of Armstrong over a group of gunsmiths over a large area.

Preceding page and right:

30. GEORGE SCHREYER (attributed). York School, Hanover, Pa. George Schreyer, whose work has been noted under the York School (No. 26) worked in Hanover which is south of York and near Emmitsburg. He was the master when John Armstrong was the pupil before the turn of the century. He influenced not only the Emmitsburg and Maryland Schools but also the school of gunsmiths in Virginia where the Schreyer shape can be seen in the stocks, butt plates and trigger guards. A Schreyer signature which cannot be seen in these pictures is a flower carved in relief on the bottom of the forestock behind the ramrod socket. Length overall 56⅝ in., bbl. 40½ in., .44 cal., rifled.

31. JOHN ARMSTRONG (signed on the barrel). Emmitsburg, Md. John Armstrong is known to have worked at his trade between 1808 and 1841. This early gun shows the strong influence of George Schreyer right down to the relief-carved flower which Armstrong copied on the underside of the forestock. He signed his own name, however, in two places, once on an inlaid brass plate on the top barrel flat and again (initials) on the lock plate. Length overall 61 in., bbl. 45 in., .49 cal., smoothbore.

32. JOHN ARMSTRONG (signed on the barrel). Emmitsburg, Md. Armstrong became one of the most prolific of the Kentucky rifle makers. Many of his details repeat again and again but the quality was kept high. The rifle illustrated, the third down, represents a high mean of Armstrong production dating from the 1820s. The gun is practical and at the same time it is handsome. Unlike so many of the gunsmiths who built Kentuckys, Armstrong was of English descent. In addition to having four sons, all of whom he trained as gunsmiths, he also trained Nathaniel Rowe. Armstrong was a fine engraver and wood carver who sacrificed inventiveness in order to get production. The heart in the teardrop back of the lock and the large, nearly round cheek piece inlay with a fine Armstrong-engraved American eagle are personal touches. Length overall 58½ in., bbl. 42⅝ in., .42 cal., rifled.

33. NATHANIEL ROWE. (signed on the barrel). Emmitsburg, Md.

Rowe, who was trained by Armstrong, became a master gunsmith in turn and built beautiful and high quality guns in Emmitsburg for many years. He is supposed to have lived to be ninety-three years old. Many Armstrong touches are apparent in a comparison of the two lower guns. The high comb with nice relief-carved detail, the shape of the patch box and its piercing, the strong curve of the butt plate and the large, nearly round cheek piece insert with the American eagle are all Armstrong touches. Length overall 59⅞ in., bbl. 44 in., .43 cal., rifled.

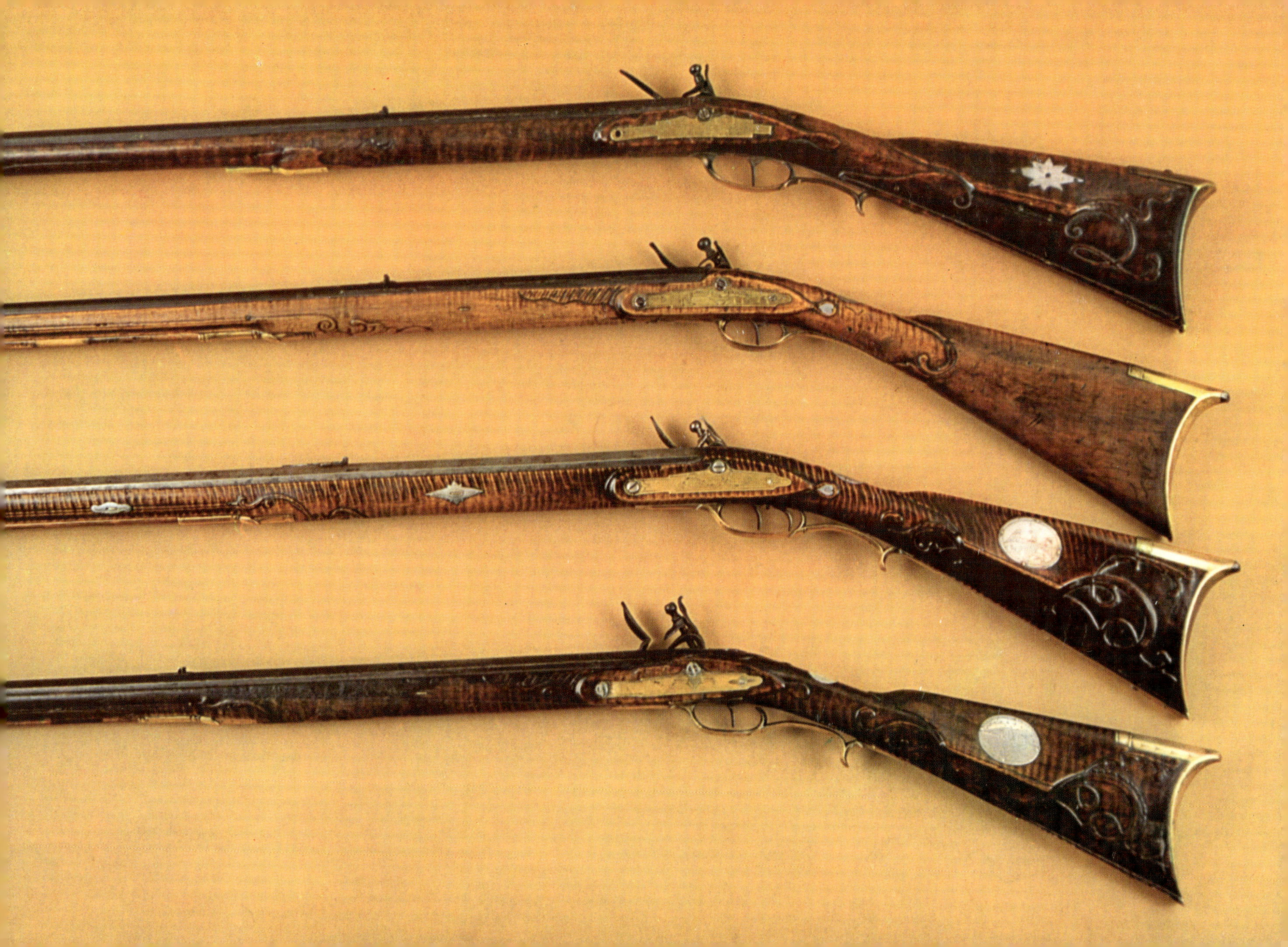

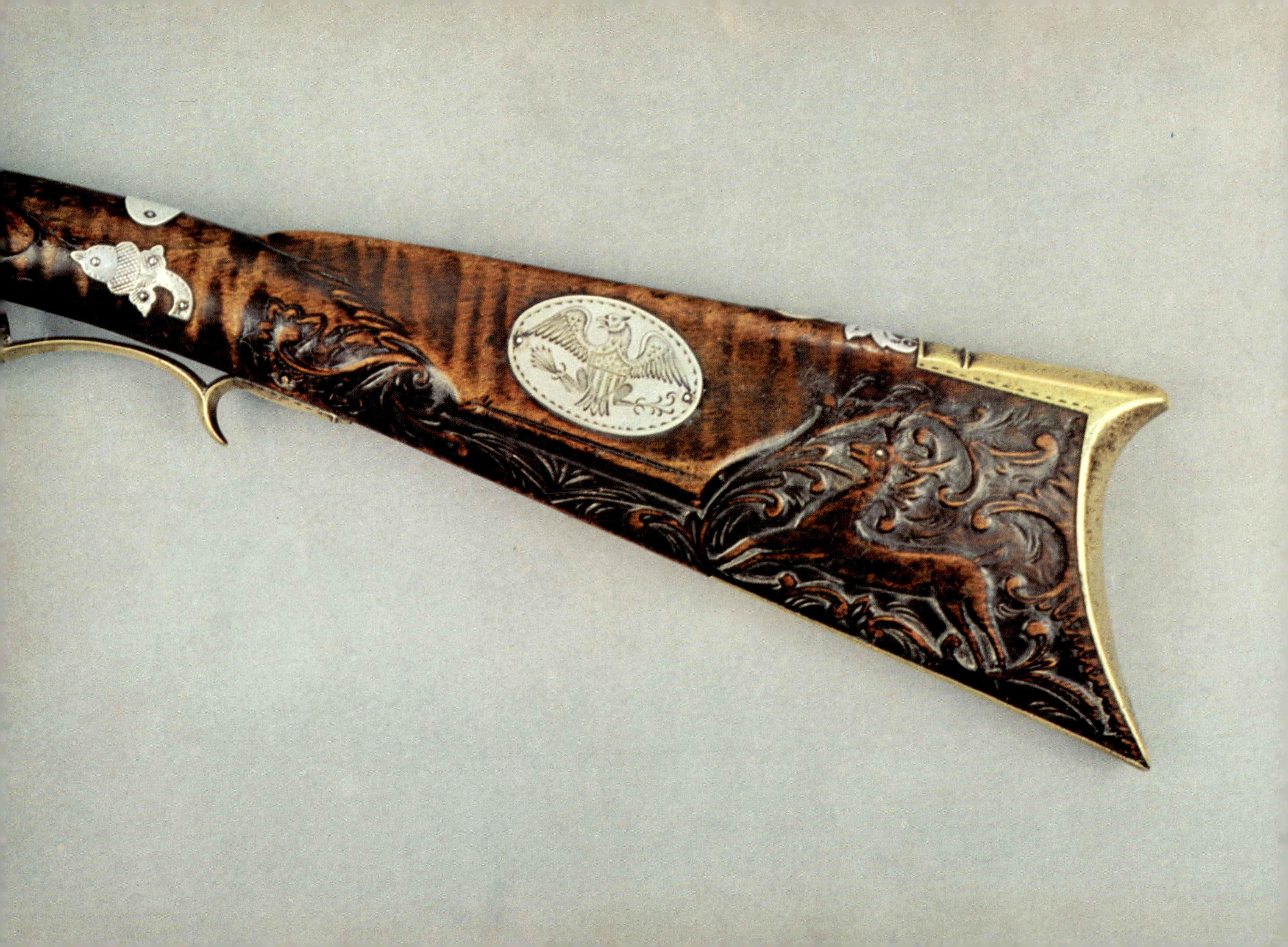

11. The Chambersburg School

The Chambersburg School utilized many details popular with the Emmitsburg gunsmiths to the southeast and forecast others found frequently on guns from Bedford and west. Architecturally, Kentuckys made in the Chambersburg area are long and slender with straight though not especially high combs. The stocks are straight and have an extreme drop. Their generally well-designed and executed relief carving varies to such an extent that no detail can be cited as typical of the area. Side plates of identical outline appear repeatedly on Chambersburg rifles. The symmetrical S-scroll design engraved in variation on many of their patch box lids and side plates is an earmark of this school. Chambersburg rifles bear a number of silver inlays, beautifully engraved and sometimes pierced.

Although the Nolls, John and Henry, are known to have worked in this area, their guns display none of the characteristics associated with this school.

Left: Detail of No. 35.

Overleaf, top to bottom:

34. JOHN NOLL (signed on barrel). Chambersburg, Pa. John Noll's father was probably a gunsmith in Lancaster County. A study of his work would indicate that the son learned his trade in Reading and York, possibly working with Conrad Welshans of York. He made rifles, pistols and swords in Washington Township, Franklin County, between 1800 and 1820. He had a fondness for the use of birds in decoration and sometimes uses a sword as a trade mark. This rifle is one of his finest, made for his gunsmith son. The thumb plate is engraved with the initials H.N. for Henry Noll. Length overall 56⅞ in., bbl. 41 in., .45 cal., rifled.

35. CHRISTIAN BECK (signed on the barrel). Chambersburg, Pa. Christian Beck, III, the nephew of J. P. Beck, (Nos. 4 and 19) learned gunsmithing from Andrew Figthorn of Womelsdorf, Reading school. The running deer which Beck carved on the stock at the left is atypical of the Chambersburg school. The bright cutting of the cheek oval, the acorns on the throat and the elaborate silver inlays on the forestock are Chambersburg characteristics. Length overall 55$\frac{15}{16}$ in., bbl. 40⅛ in., .38 cal., rifled.

36. CHRISTIAN BECK (barrel signed C. Beck). Chambersburg, Pa. This is a late Beck rifle. The large patch box and the silver fore end inlays follow the earlier rifle. Length overall 57 in., bbl. 41½ in., .38 cal., rifled.

Detail of No. 35 (top) & No. 34 (bottom) fore end inlays.

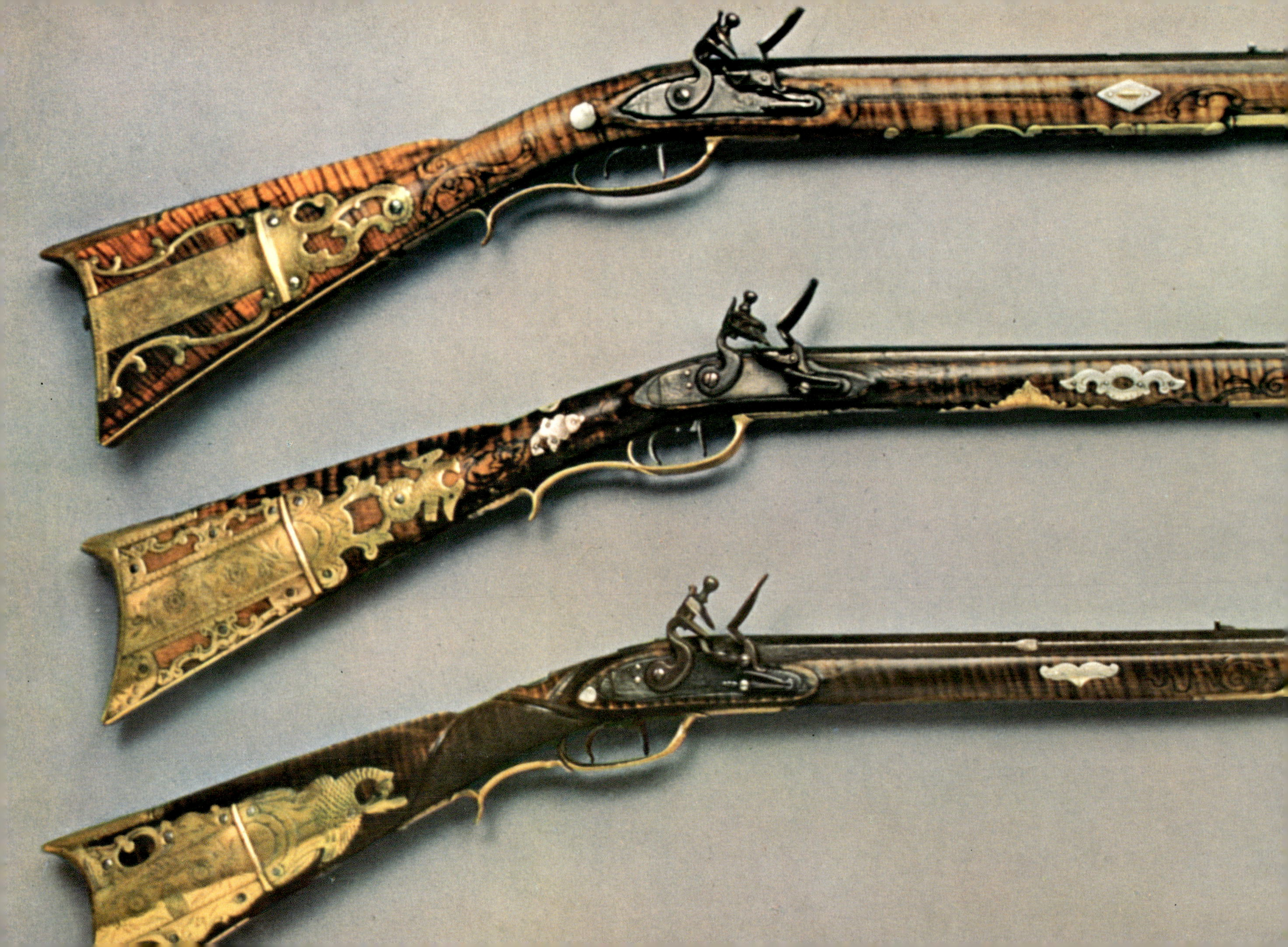

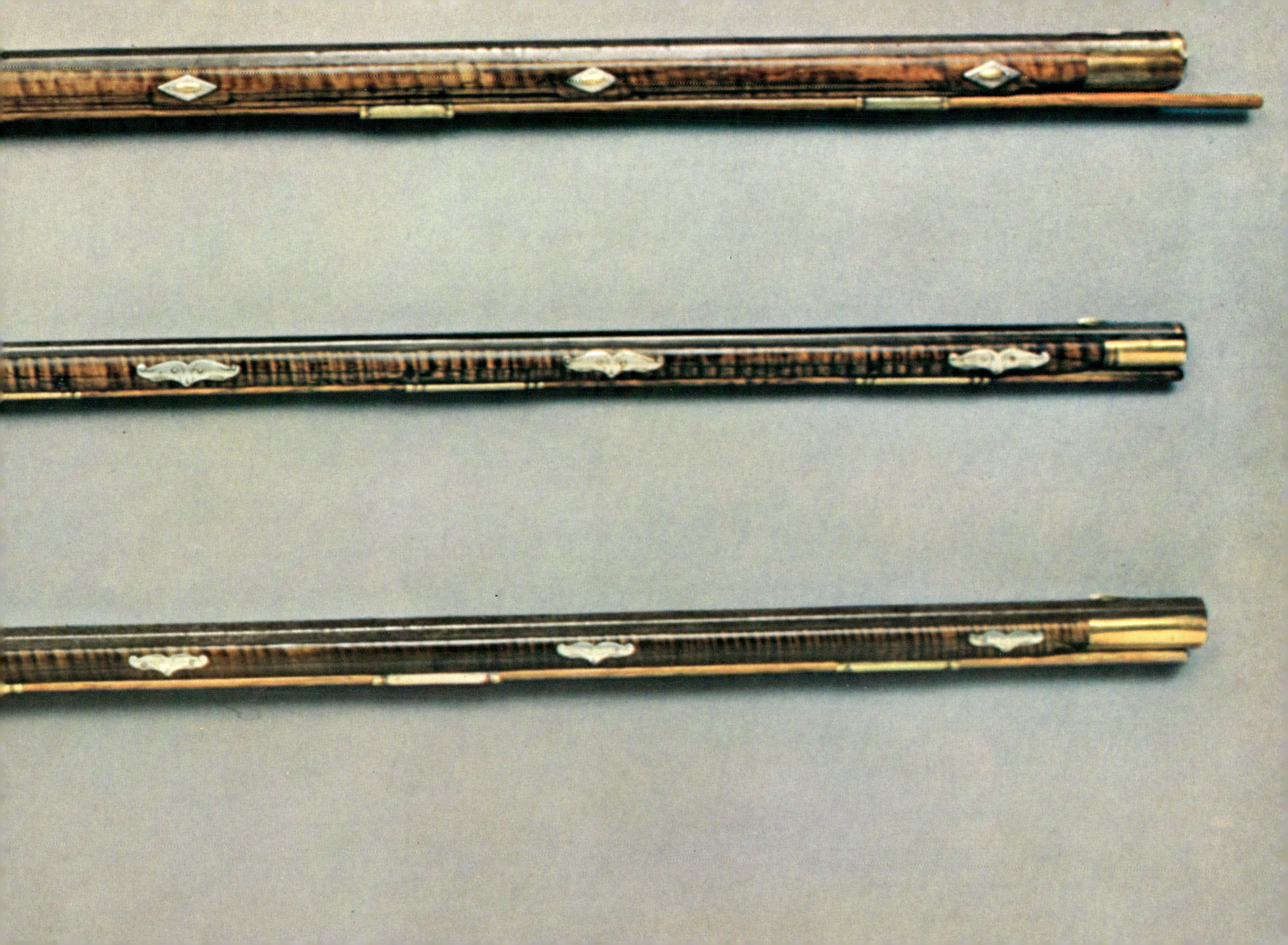

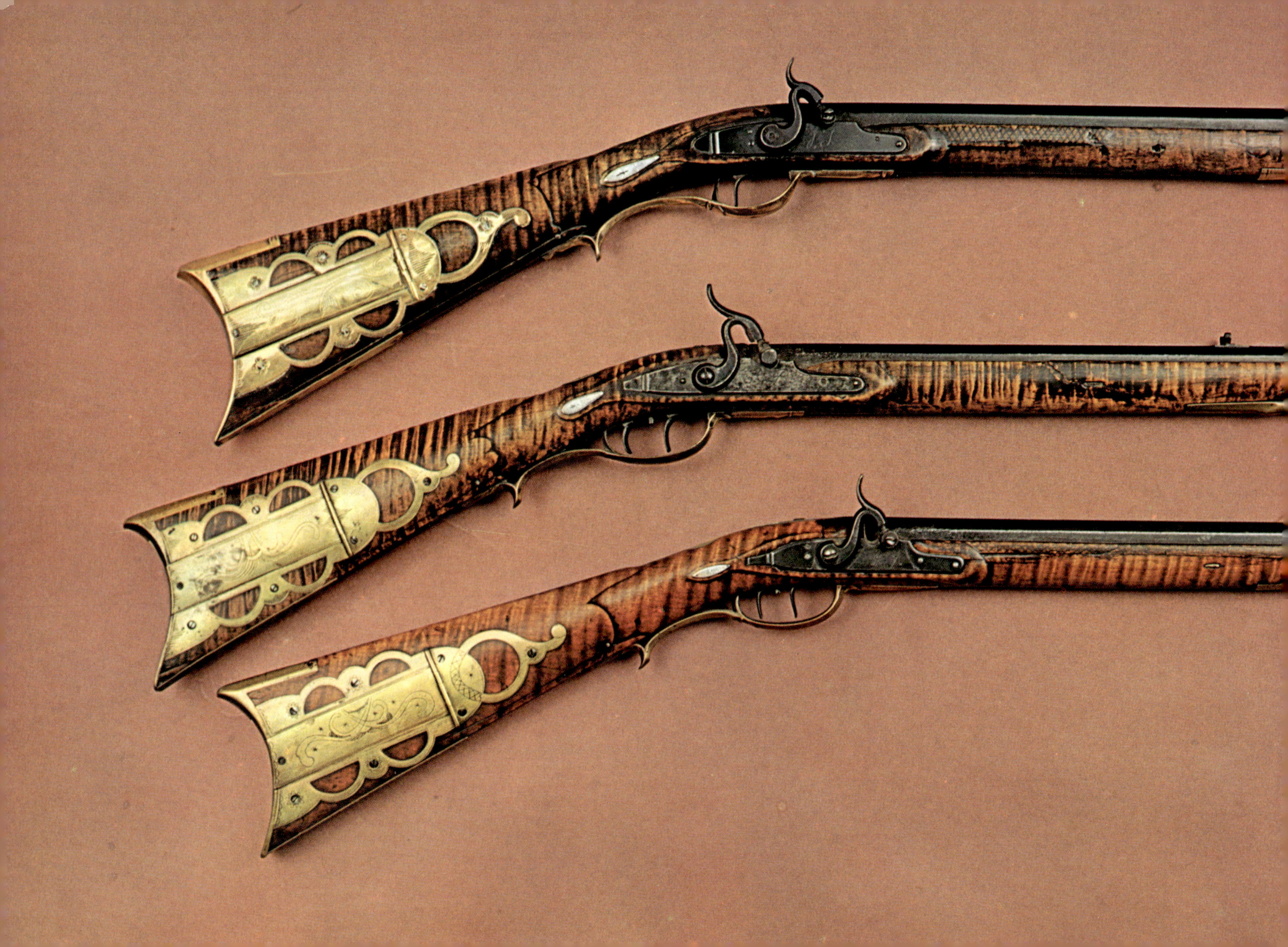

12. The Bedford School

The gunsmiths of this area produced an unusually delicate, light rifle architecturally that is not likely to be confused with the rifles of the schools east of Bedford. They are actually typical of the relatively late period and are quite frequently percussion. The cameo cutting at the throat and the buttstocks with their pronounced drop, a long, straight comb and a narrow, thin butt are identifying characteristics.

The four-part engraved patch box with a ring, the Bedford side plate and the lozenge-shaped inlay in the throat are characteristic of this area and might be thought of as a simpler stylization of the earlier types of the schools to the east. Likewise, relief carving was carried to a rather late date and was a highly stylized interpretation of the earlier rococo.

Graceful hand forged locks were quite common to this school and are recognized by the tapered, squared off rear extension of the lock plate and the long curved neck of the hammer.

Preceding page and right:

37. JACOB STOUDENOUR (signed with initials "J.S." on the barrel and on the hand-forged lock plate). Bedford, Pa.

Joseph Mills, J. Fraizer, Peter White and Jacob Stoudenour (1795-1863) were pioneer gunsmiths in Bedford. All three built flintlocks for a brief period before percussion took over. This percussion rifle exhibits all of the typical Bedford features, the graceful cock, lock with set triggers made by the gunsmith, the silver teardrop inlay behind the lock, the cameo throat carving and the pierced segments of circles (loop and hook) surrounding the patch box cover. Length overall 57$\frac{9}{16}$ in., bbl. 42$\frac{5}{16}$ in., .43 cal., rifled.

38. AMOS, BORDER & CO. (signed with initials "A & B x CO." on the barrel and "A.B." on the lock plate). Bedford, Pa.

Kentucky's rifles, if signed, usually gave the name of an individual gunsmith, not that of a company. This signature is the result of a partnership between two gunsmiths who handmade all of the parts of their guns in an age when Yankee gunsmiths such as Colt were stamping out parts by the thousands. The isolation of Bedford in the ranges of the Alleghenies made the Bedford gunsmiths self-reliant. John Amos (1800-1867) and Daniel B. Border (1826-1891) worked together for many years producing fine guns like this one. Note the double set triggers with the adjustment screw for trigger pull between the two triggers. The spur on the hammer, while the most exaggerated of these three Bedford guns, is well designed for quick retraction by the shooter's thumb. The lock, throat and cock work well in the trigger hand. An elaborate rifle for such a late period, it has simple engraving on the side plate, a good American eagle cut in the silver cheek piece inlay and continues the relief carving of an earlier period on the left stock, back of the cheek piece. Length overall 58¼ in., bbl. 43¼ in., 34 cal., rifled.

39. WILLIAM DEFIBAUGH (signed in script on the barrel, dated "1854" on the side plate). Bedford, Pa.

William Defibaugh (1814-1891) of Monroe Township had at least one son who was a gunsmith and perhaps others, as there were five Defibaughs who were gunsmiths working in Bedford County in the 19th century. Not all of William's rifles had relief carving nor did they all have the Bedford school patch box. The carving for the cameo effect on the left side of these three guns presented more of an aesthetic problem than on the right side because of the conflicting planes of the cheek piece. This is partly solved in the Defibaugh piece by the descending steps carved in the stock below the cheek piece oval insert. Length overall 59⅞ in., bbl. 44½ in., .34 cal., rifled. Note the small calibre of the later Bedford pieces. This was due both to the improvement of the powder and the decrease of large game and Indians.

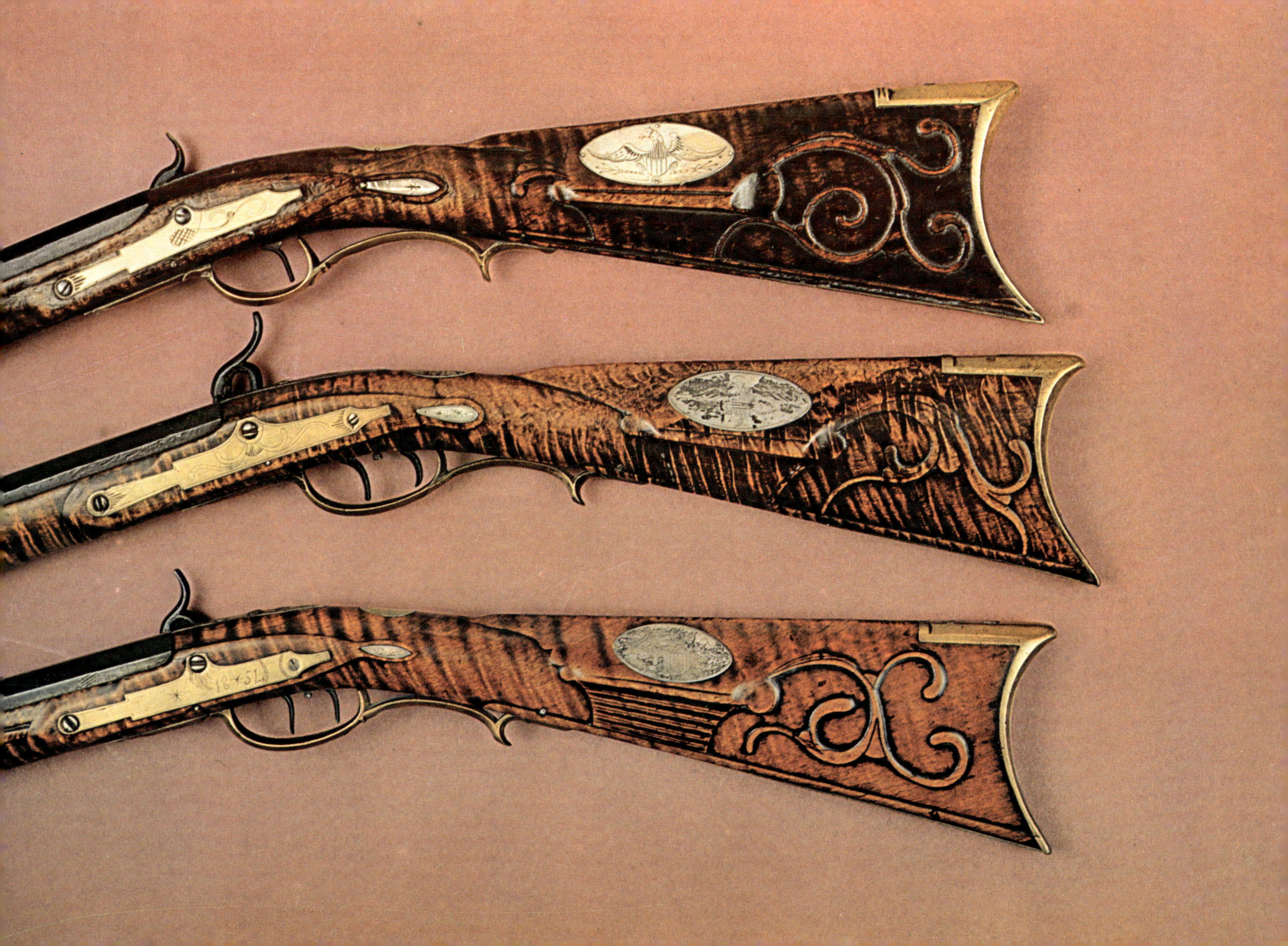

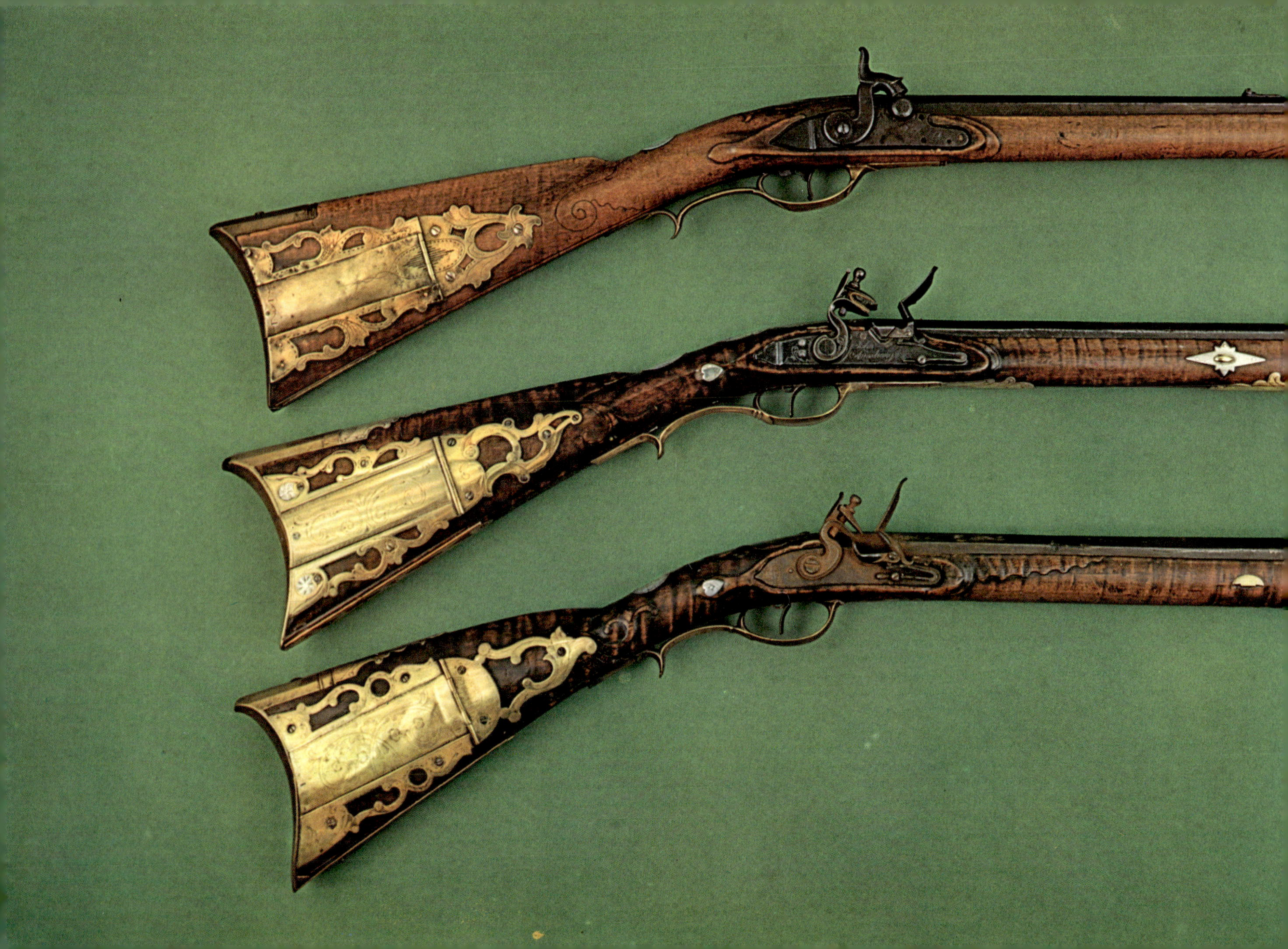

13. The Maryland School

The Maryland School of gunsmithing was directly influenced by the York School and follows closely much of the artistic ornamentation but with refinements that distinguished it as a school on its own.

Architecturally, the guns made in the Emmitsburg, Hagerstown and Frederick areas were long, slender rifles stocked usually in highly figured curly Maple with a thin wrist, wide flaring buttstock and fine forestock mouldings. The wrists were long with a pronounced curve from the tang to the comb. The lower edge of the buttstock were frequently moulded.

The patch boxes were large with from three to five perforations and the finials were usually in the form of a flower. Very frequently, some of the elements of carving are repeated in the highly refined engraving. A feature not usually found in the rifles of other areas is the addition of an extra screw near the tail end of the side plates which secures the plate after the lock bolts have been removed.

Occasionally, hand forged locks are found on rifles in this school and are frequently distinctive in being engraved.

Left, top to bottom:

40. J. GROVE (signed on barrel). Hagerstown, Md.
No one knows what relationship there may have been between Samuel Grove and his son, both gunsmiths in York, Pa., and this Hagerstown maker. In any event, Grove was one of the early Maryland gunsmiths and this is a rare and early piece from the Hagerstown area, with its long slender wrist and flaring stock. This otherwise fine piece has been subjected to a typical conversion to percussion. The touchhole has been bored out to accept a nipple drum and the flintlock cock has been replaced with a percussion hammer. The hole for the frizzen spring screw can be seen in the illustration.

41. JOHN ARMSTRONG (signed on the barrel and lock plate). Emmitsburg, Md.
This Kentucky is the finest of all the great rifles known to be made by the Emmitsburg master. Two other of his rifles have been shown earlier in the Emmitsburg section (Nos. 31 and 32). This piece has all of the plusses that are dear to a Kentucky rifle collector's heart. In addition to the fine architecture and workmanship, there are many silver inlays which look like they belong to the gun and have not just been pasted on for gaudy effect. Note the decorative brass frame around the cheek inlay. Length overall 62¾ in., bbl. 46¾ in., .45 cal., rifled.

42. FREDERICK STOVER (signed on the barrel). Emmitsburg school.
Stover is known to have been working in the years between 1800 and 1826. He was probably not around as long as his contemporary Andrew Kopp, who was born in 1782 and lived until 1875! Both men and John Armstrong drank from the same well, although the relief carving on the stock varies in the work of all three makers shown. Length overall 57 in., bbl. 41$\frac{13}{16}$ in., .50 cal., smoothbore.

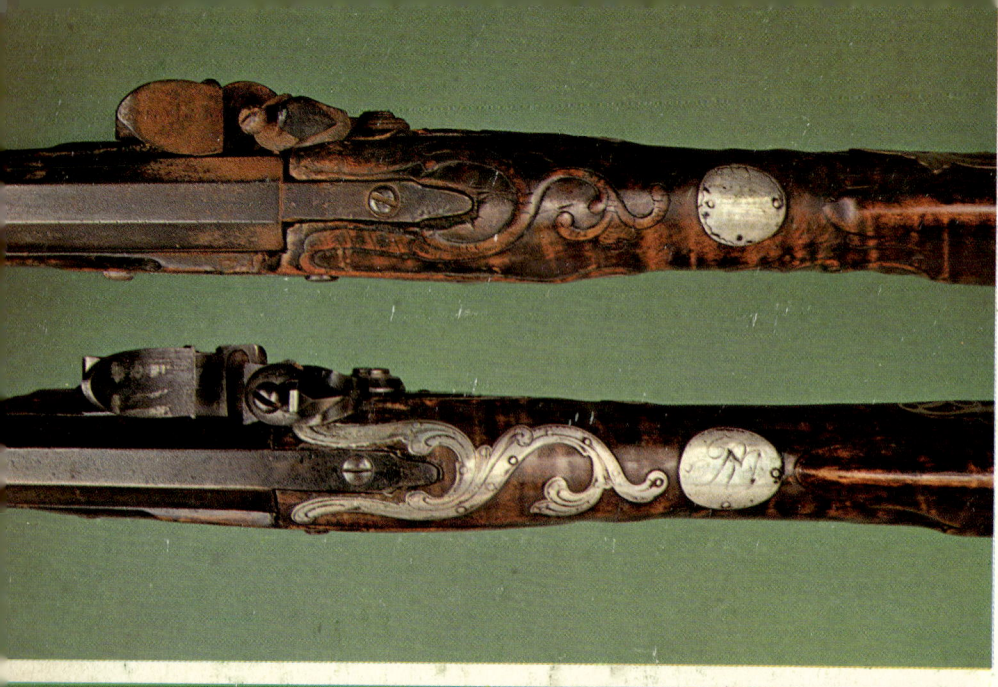

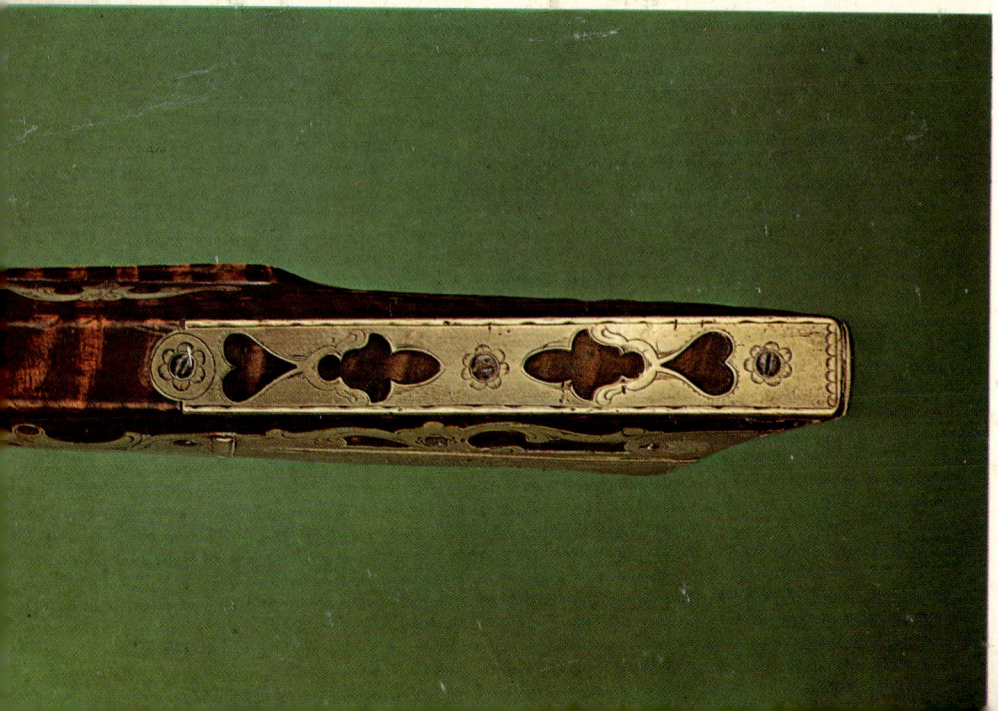

Right: Reverse of Nos. 40, 41 & 42.

Left, above: Repeat design in silver and wood of Nos. 41 & 42.

Left, below: Detail of toe piece of No. 41. The heart-shaped inlays are an Armstrong signature.

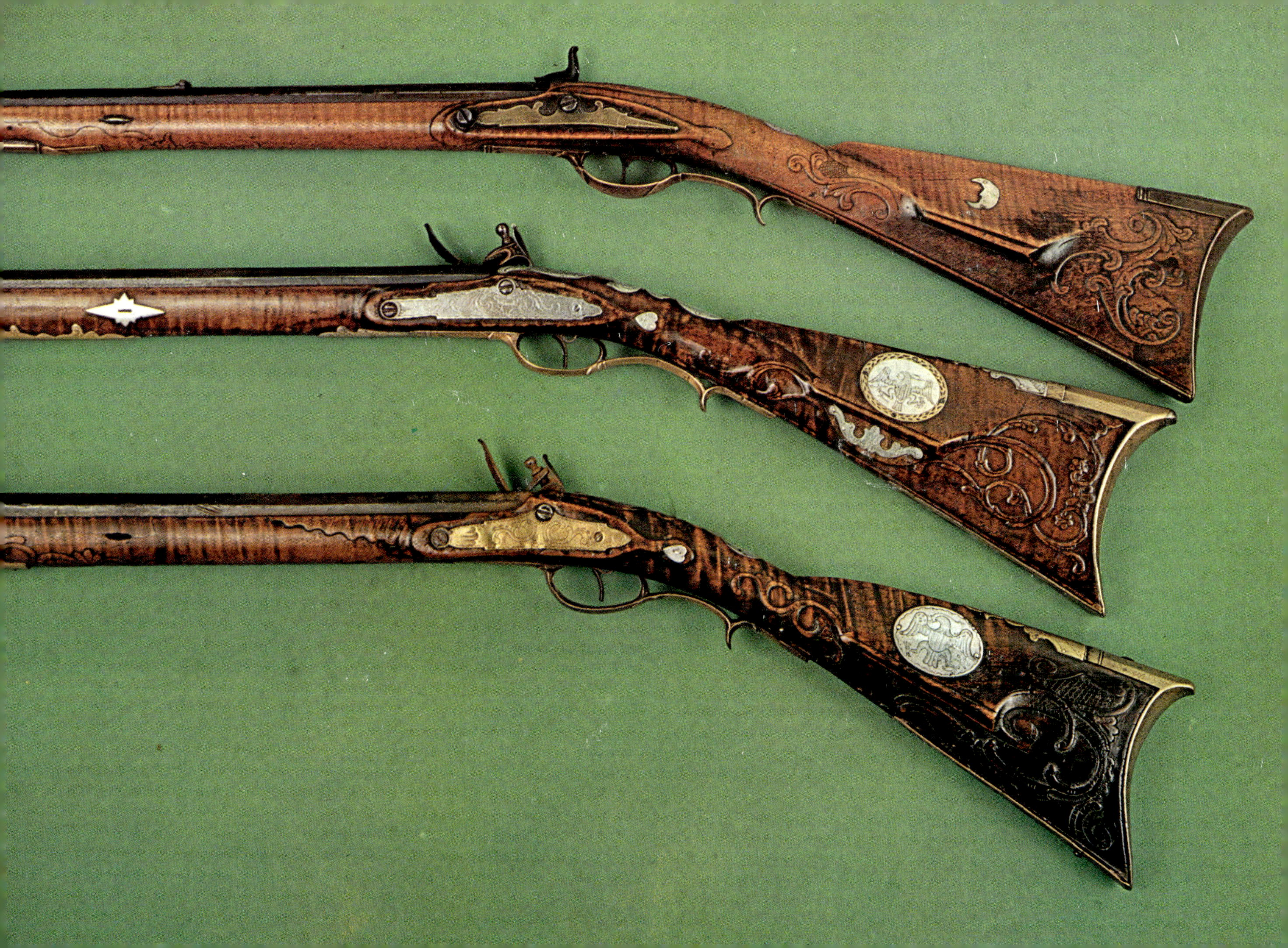

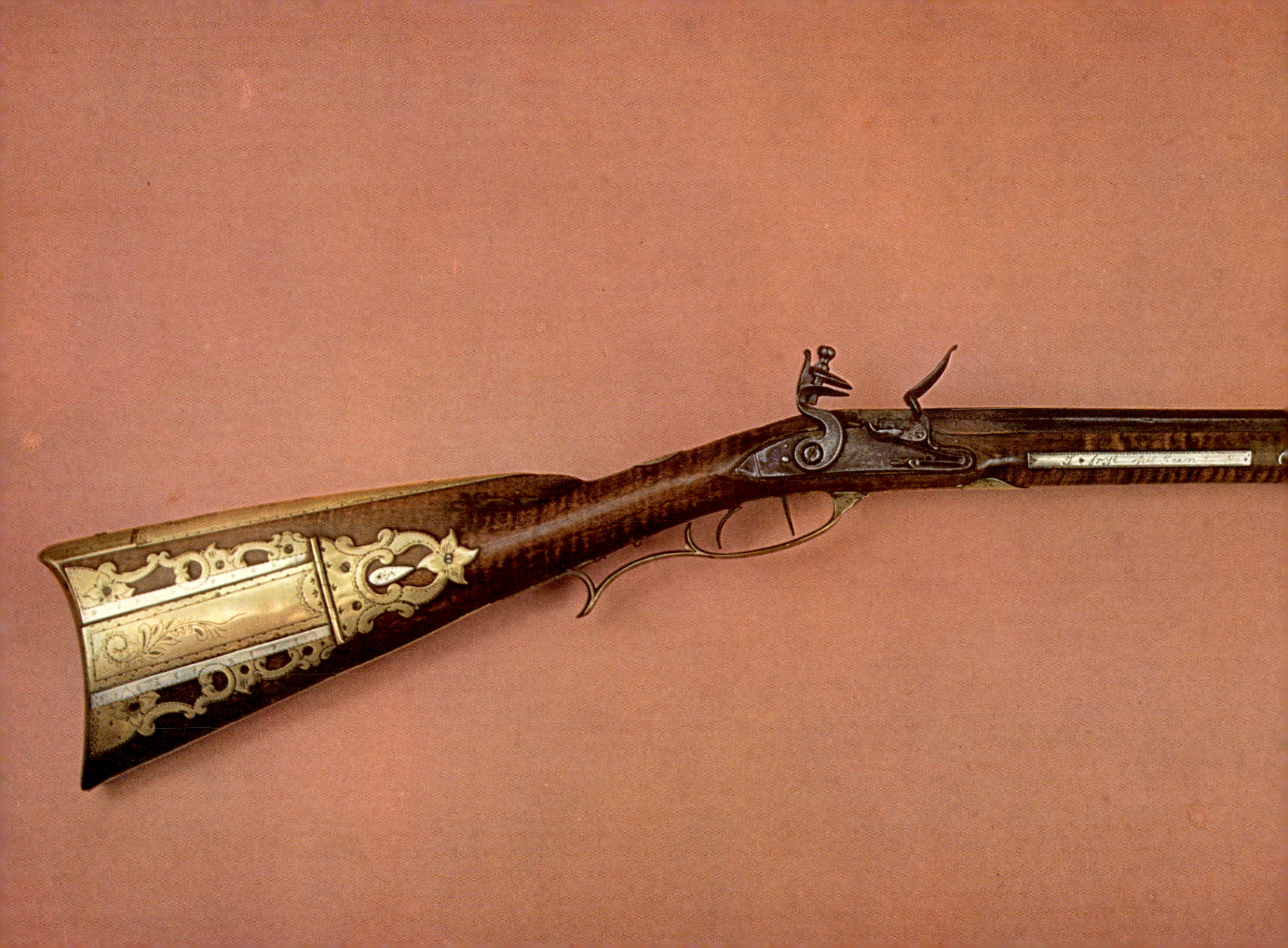

14. *The Virginia School*

The Winchester School in the Frederick County area influenced rifles made in Virginia more than did any other school. They are characterized by having a greater mass than the average Pennsylvania-made gun. A trained eye will observe their well proportioned bigness. In handling Virginia rifles, considerably more heft will be noted.

At least fifteen or twenty gunsmiths were working in this area before the Revolution. The Winchester school influenced rifles made down the Shenandoah Valley into North Carolina and westward through the Cumberland Gap. It also had a significant influence on rifles made through the Potomac Valley and Monongahela Valley to Pittsburgh. The Winchester school produced finer rifles from an artistic standpoint than were made in any of the other Virginia schools.

The second most significant area of rifle production in Virginia was the James River Basin School. Documents place the beginning of this school in the 1750s. The influence of this school on North Carolina and Southwestern Virginia was stronger than the Winchester School and was felt on East Tennessee Rifles.

Left and right: 43. SIMON LAUCK (signed on the barrel). Winchester, Va.
This sturdy Virginia rifle is a handsome piece with its finely engraved brass and silver patch box and brass reinforcement over the comb. Silver plates on either side of the forestock are engraved with the legend: "S. Frye his gun" and "G. Wilkin". The sword, silver moon cutting into the edge of a brass sun and the legend *The Sunin Cleps*, "The Sun in eclipse", on the left stock, is a message from the gunsmith. The rifle was undoubtedly made in the year 1806 when there was a major eclipse on the eastern Atlantic seaboard which would have been partial in Virginia. Length overall 60⅝ in., bbl. 44⅜ in., .56 cal., rifled.

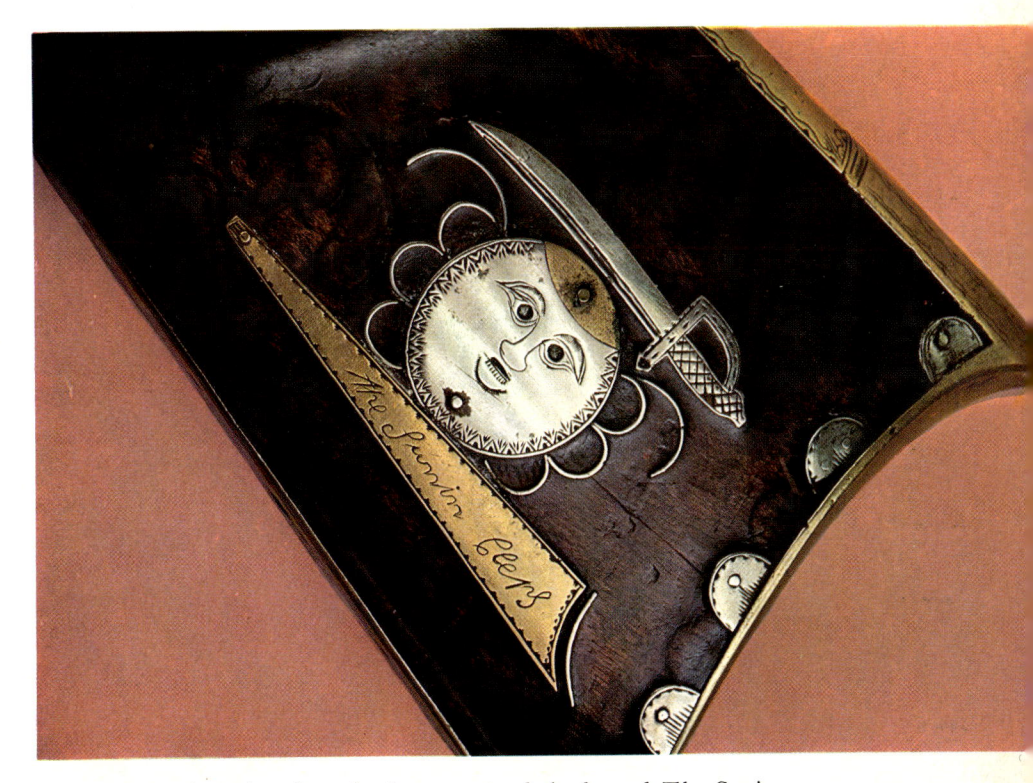

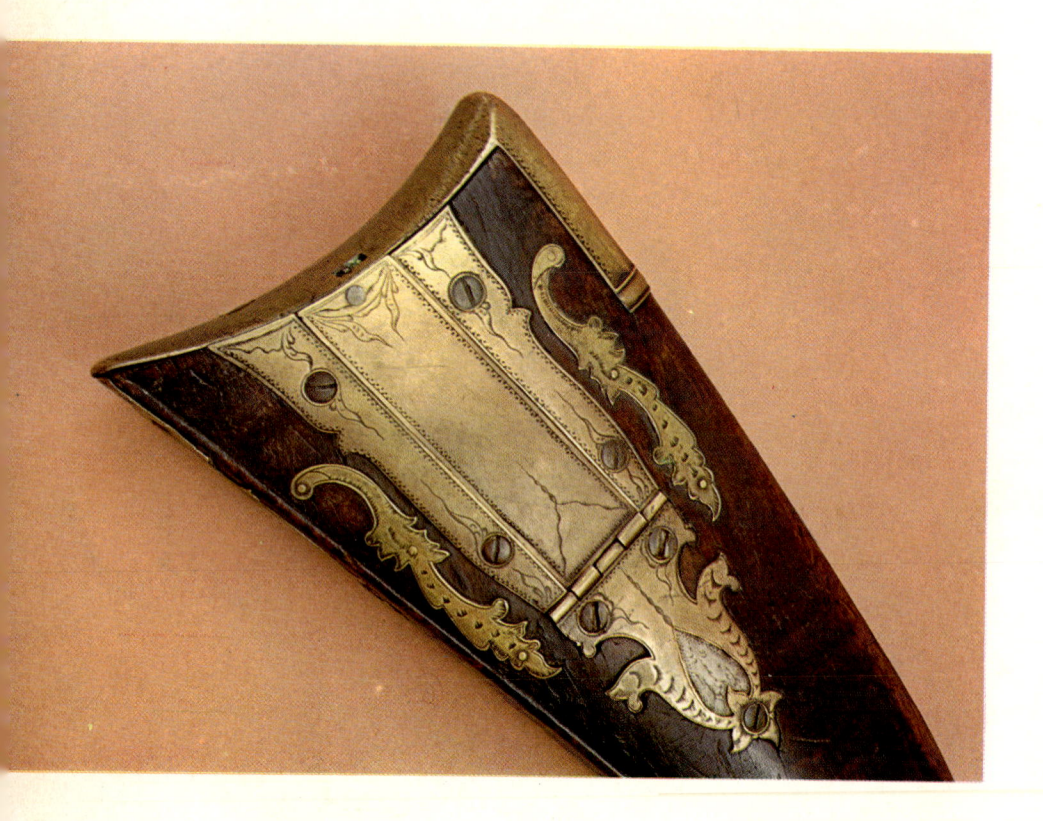

Left: Detail of patch box of No. 44. CHRISTIAN HUFFMAN (signed on barrel). Woodstock, Shenandoah County, Va.

C. Huffman was old enough to be married in 1782 and therefore was old enough to have completed his apprenticeship and started as a gunsmith. He was still working at his craft in 1805 according to a surviving deed which shows his occupation. He was not only a fine gunsmith but a creative artist as can be seen in this illustration of the patch box of one of his guns. Here silver and brass have not only been combined in a subtle fashion, but the understated and sensitive work of the burin creates a decadent grace. The rifle is also relief carved which is rare for a Virginia piece, there being less than forty known. Length overall 62⅓ in., bbl. 46¼ in., .46 cal., rifled.

Right: 45. JACOB SHAFFER (attributed). Wythe County, Va.

This sturdily stocked and heavy barrelled target rifle made for bench or rest shooting is nevertheless graceful. It is exceptionally well made for a target rifle and has top quality engraving done on the nicely pierced patch box hardware. The butt plate return is continued visually with three inlays. The many silver inlays are decoratively engraved as is the cutout side plate. The trigger guard with its widened spur and tendril offshoots provided additional finger holds and therefore greater stability for the target shooter. This detail is also a characteristic of the Wythe school. Length overall 60⅝ in., bbl. 44⅜ in., .56 cal., rifled.

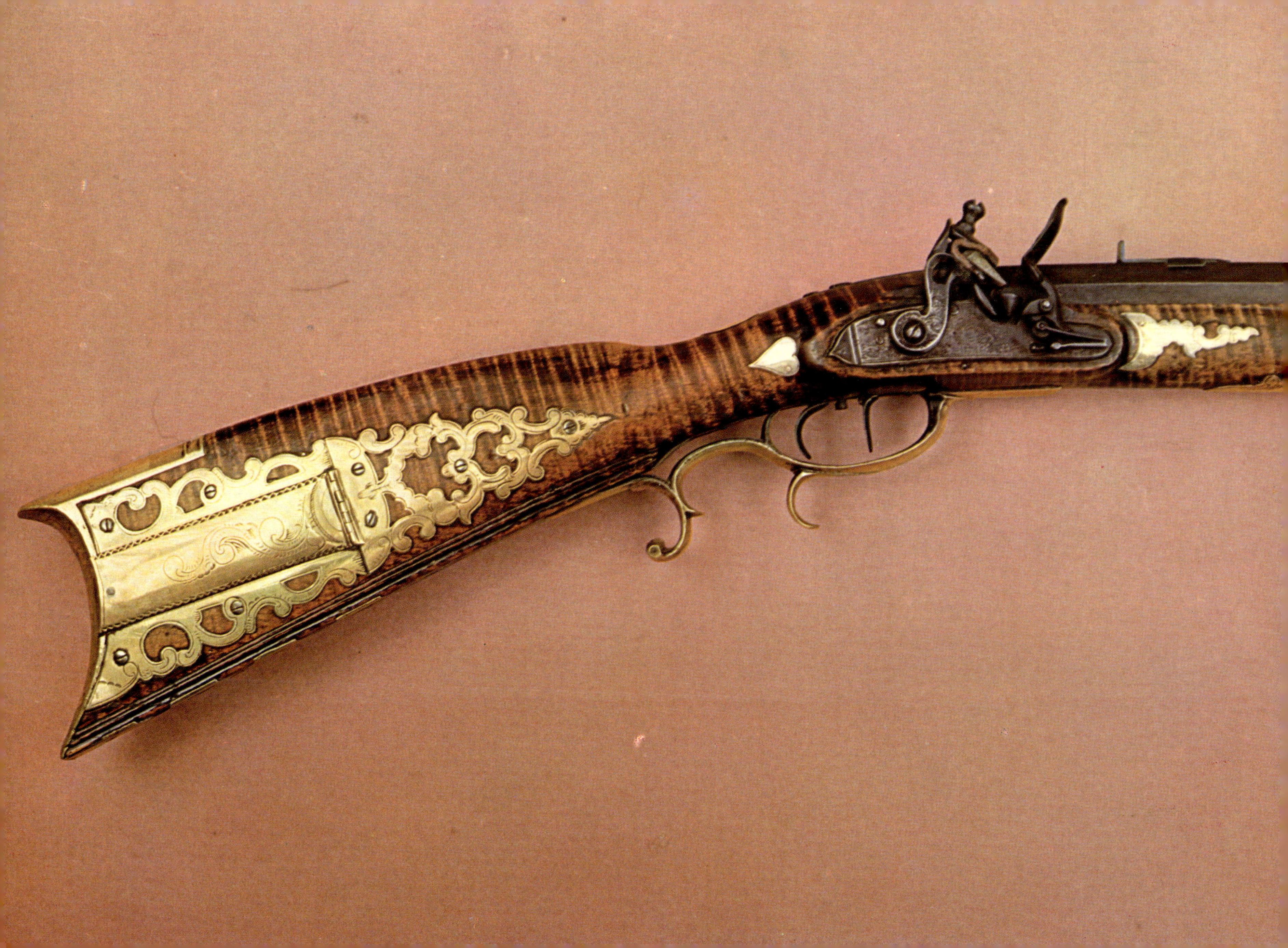

Left, above: Detail of acorns and star in silver wire and sheet silver on cheek piece of:

46. J. MONTAGUE (signed on the barrel). Winchester, Va.
We don't know where this gunsmith worked, but judging by the architecture and details such as the shape of the buttstock and other features not shown in this detail illustration, Montague must have been influenced by George Schreyer of Hanover, Pa. This influence is seen in the work of gunsmiths in the Martinsburg and Winchester areas. The rifle has a removable fore end held in place with barrel keys, and decorated with silver barrel key escutcheon plates. The silver cheek piece decoration is most unusual with its four silver acorn cutouts and the large flattened silver star inlaid on an unusually deep cheek. The silver wire inlay, common on English firearms, reflects the close cultural ties between the Virginia colony and the parent country. The length of the whole gun is 60⅝ in., bbl. 44½ in., .43 cal., rifled.

Left, below: Detail of the lock plate of 47. F. KLETTE (signed on the lock). Stevensburg, Va.
This is a detail of a fine pre-Revolutionary Virginia rifle. The period of its manufacture is shown by the trigger construction, the trigger guard shape and the shell carving around the barrel tang. The patch box assembly is also typical of the 1765-1775 period, with its wide squat appearance. The top barrel flat has the name "Sevensburg". There is no "Sevensburg" in Virginia, so this is probably the gunmakers attempt at Stevensburg. The Klett-(e) name is a famous one in European gunsmithing. The Klett family worked in Suhl and Salzburg between 1575 and 1692. (See M. Lindsay's *One Hundred Great Guns*, p. 278.) Length overall 59½ in., bbl. 43 9/16 in., .47 cal., rifled.

Right: Reverse of No. 45.

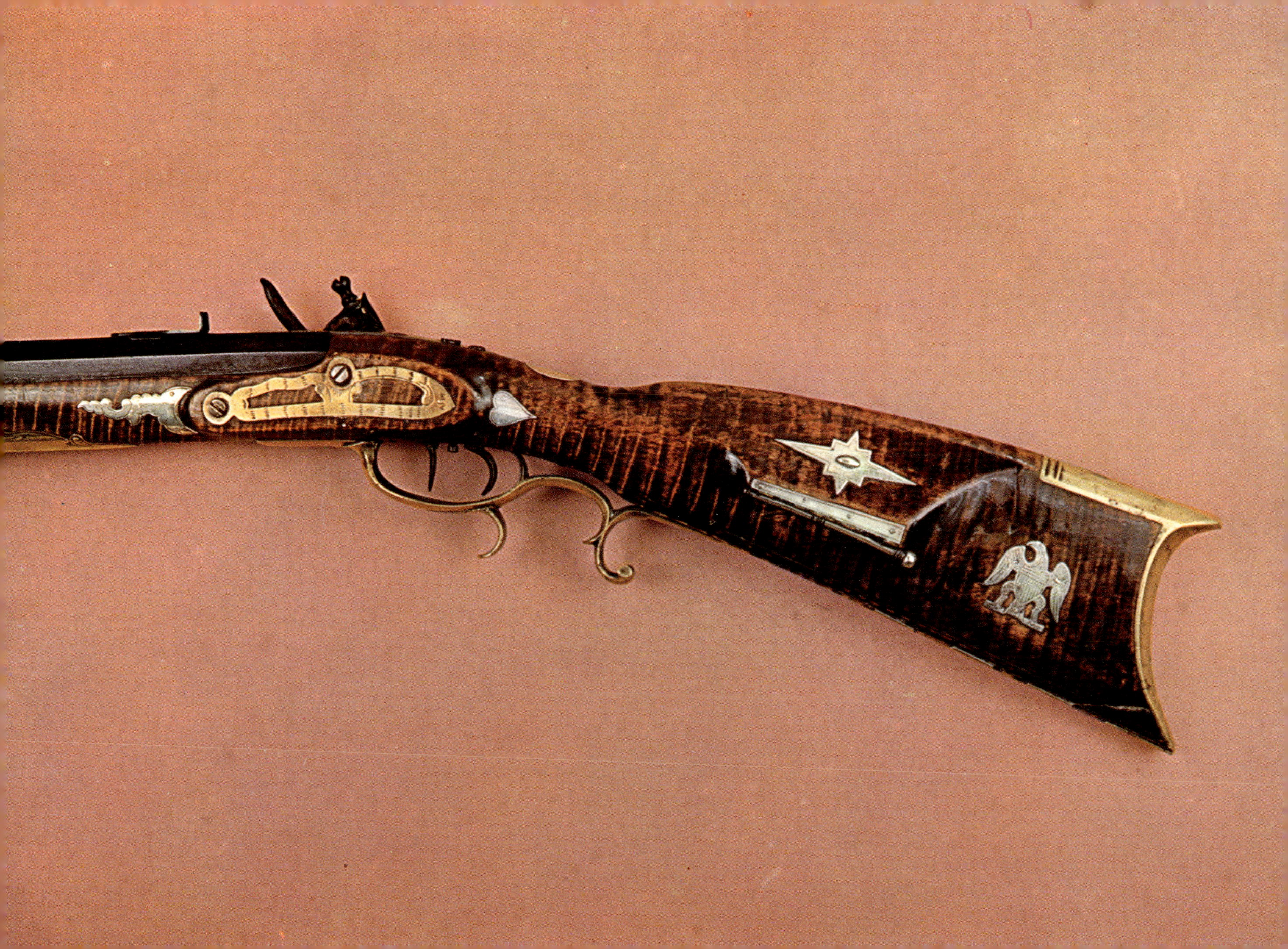

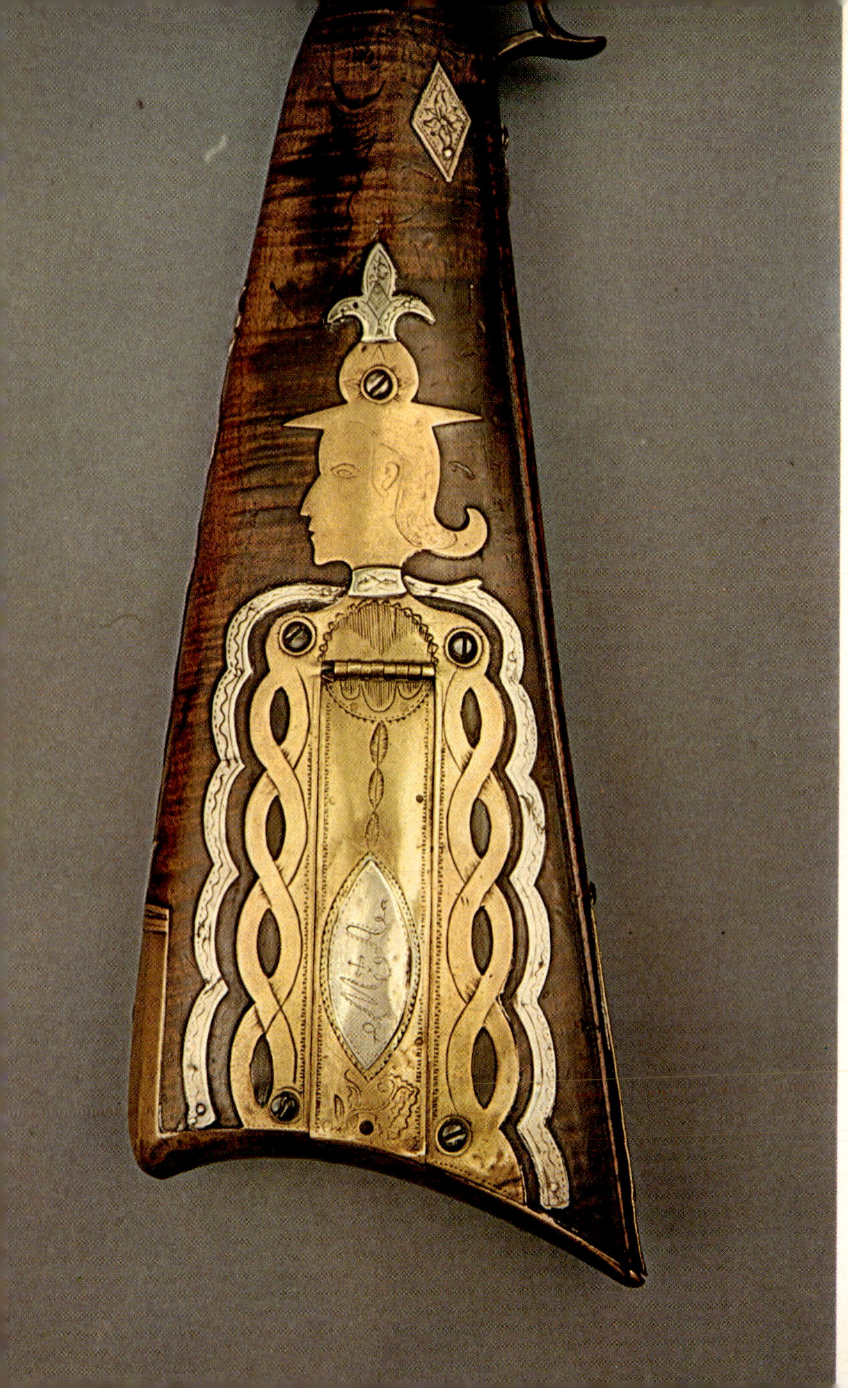

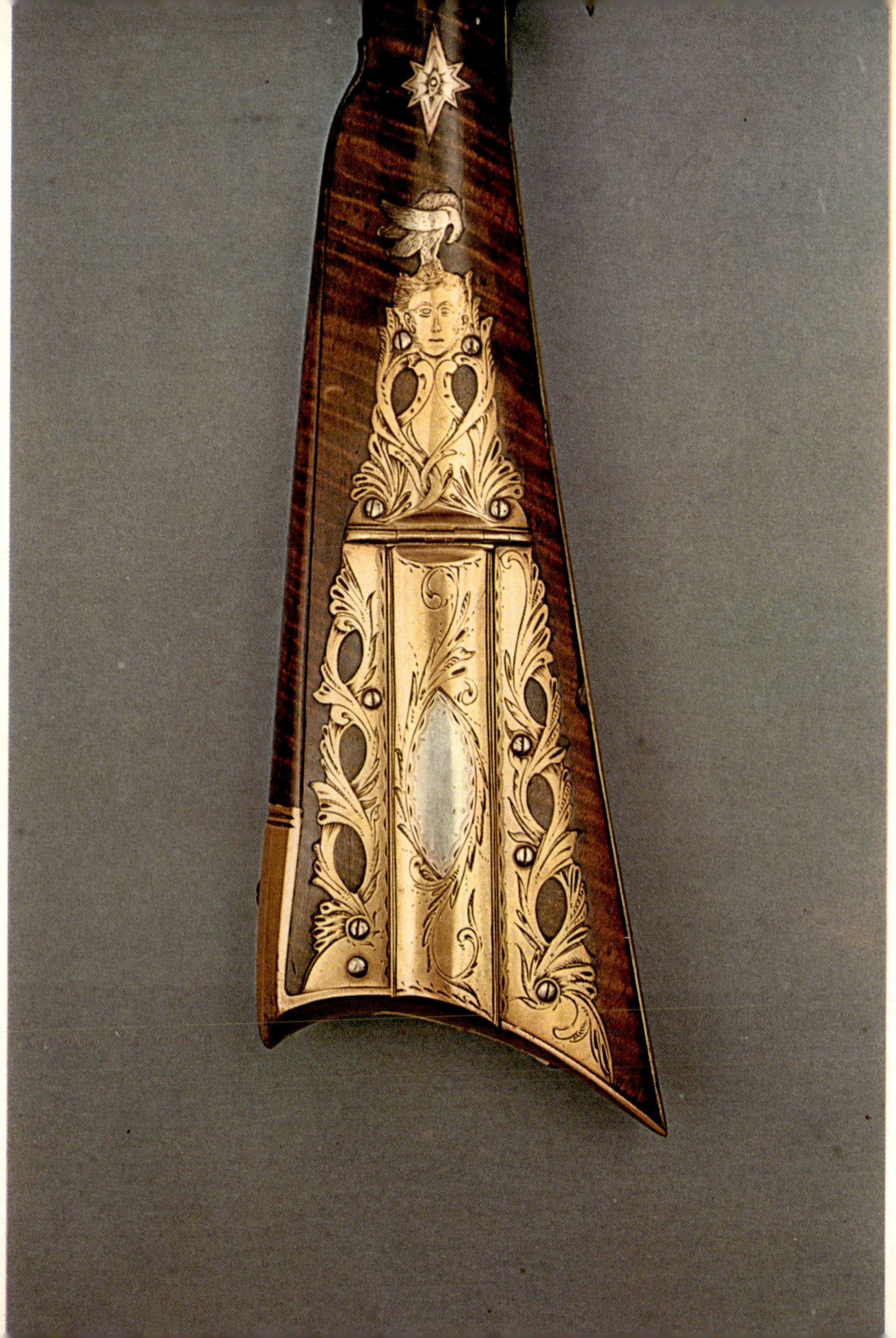

15. The North Carolina School

The long rifles made in North Carolina are both long and straight. Patch boxes are elongated and are usually signed by the maker on the patch box lid. Elliptical barrel retaining key plates are typical on the forestock as are the silver diamond-shaped inlays on the wrist of the stock. Silver bands are often inlaid on the top extentions of the butt plates.

North Carolina rifles have escaped from the rococo formalism and exhibit a pleasing naiveté in their folk art themes. The women's heads executed in silver are reminiscent of W-61 in the Winchester Gun Museum, a Georgia-made Kentucky (circa 1820), with a silver, brass and copper inlaid representation of a Southern Belle covering the patch box area.

Far left:

48. M.A. (signed on the patch box lid). Location in Carolina unknown.
The "M.A." engraved in the silver insert on the patch box cover of the rifle farthest left would seem to be the initials of the owner, but in North Carolina the patch box cover was the customary location for the maker's name. The name of the owner of this rifle appears twice; once on a silver insert in the brass side plate. Here it is misspelled "John Amss". A second try is more successful with a silver plate inlaid in the steel barrel. It says "Made for John Amoss August ye 1 + 180 (?)". The combination of silver and brass and the soldering in of silver inserts is a feature of some of the best southern-made Kentuckys. The primitive art, Grandma Moses-like, women's heads and full standing figures, have a charm and character just as the Pennsylvania folk art does on the Christian Beck and Jacob Sell rifles. Length overall 58$\frac{13}{16}$ in., bbl. 42½ in., .45 cal., rifled.

Left:

49. NATHANIEL VOGLER (signed on the barrel). Salem, N.C.
The most important gunsmiths in Salem, North Carolina, were the Vogler family. The maker of the gun on the right was Nathaniel, son of gunsmith Christopher Vogler. He was born in 1804, and this gun, the finest one extant, was made when he was in his early twenties, sometime between 1825 and 1830. The silver inlay in the brass occurs in Nathaniel's work but his drawing and engraving are more sophisticated than the work of "M.A." The lady with the choker and earrings either has the fanciest hat in North Carolina or a bird of unknown variety has chosen to sit there. On the next page there is an illustration of the bi-metal side plate of this same gun. The silver inlay is in the shape of a snake bearing the legend, "The seed of the woman hath bruised the serpent's head." Whatever it means, the gunsmith was a lot more literate than some we have run into. A silver inlay on the top of the barrel has the maker's name "Nathaniel Vogler Salem NC" while the silver inlay in the patch box cover remains blank. Length overall 62 in., bbl. 46⅛ in., .42 cal., rifled.

from OLD SALEM, Winston Salem, North Carolina

Detail of No. 49.

Right:

50. W.B. (signed on patch box lid). Rowan school.
Any fool can tell that "W.B." made fine rifles. Who he was, no one knows, but all three guns which were loaned by Old Salem to the Kentucky Rifle exhibition were made by a master gunsmith. The top rifle on the right has particularly fine relief carving around the cheek. The flattened silver star on the cheek is well executed and located. This rifle is dated 1813 on the side plate. Length overall 61¼ in., bbl. 45 3/16 in., .35 cal., rifled.

51. W.B. (signed on patch box lid). Rowan school.
This second rifle by "W.B." could be of earlier production by the unknown North Carolina master, and a third rifle, not shown, is dated 1814. The lower piece on the right makes full use of a rococo swirl with deep relief-carved tendrils to fill the area of the left side of the stock which does not come in contact with the shooter's face. The concave curve of the butt plate is almost as deep as a schuetzen rifle stock. Length overall 62 in., bbl. 45¾ in., .37 cal., rifled.

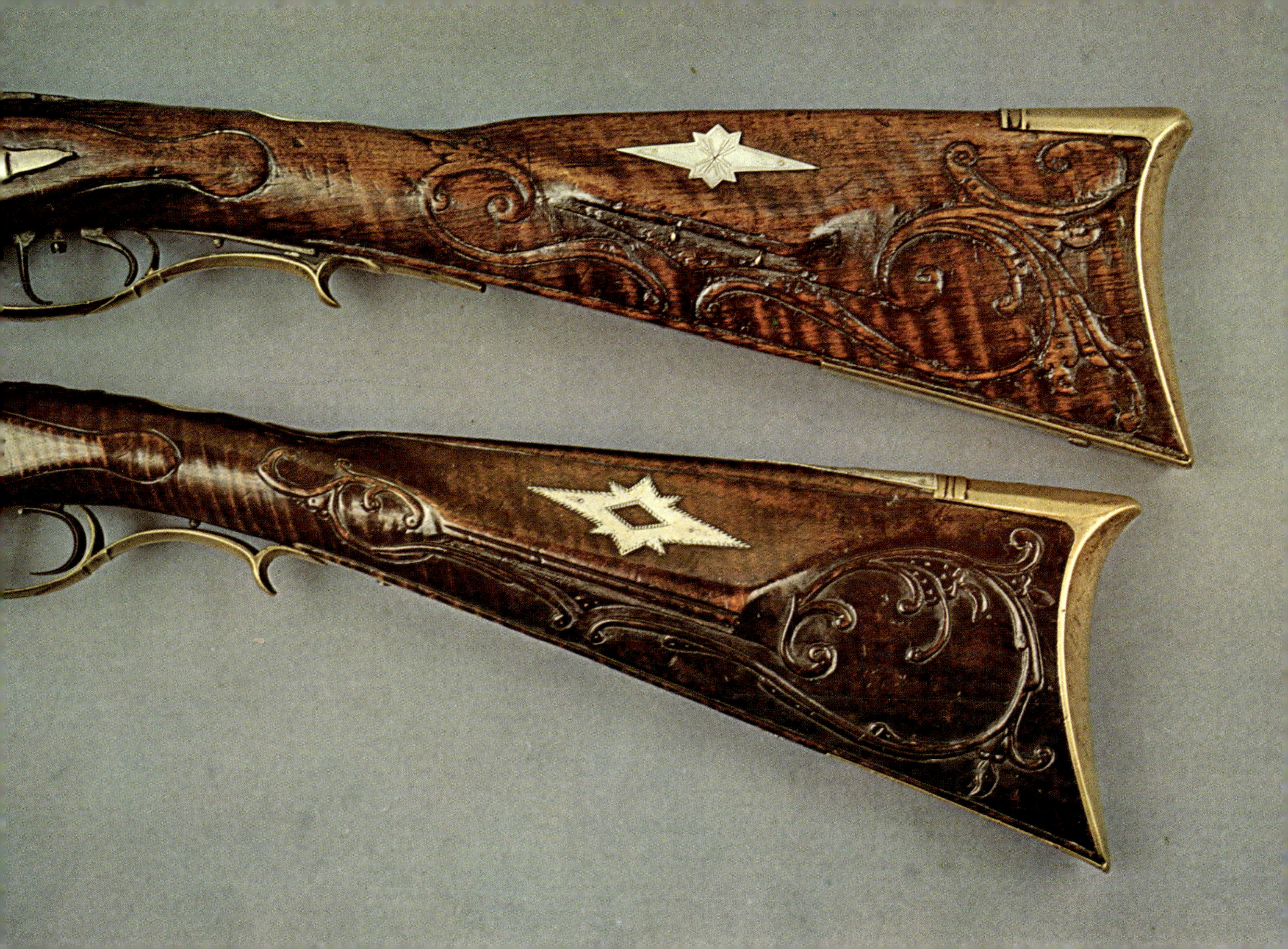

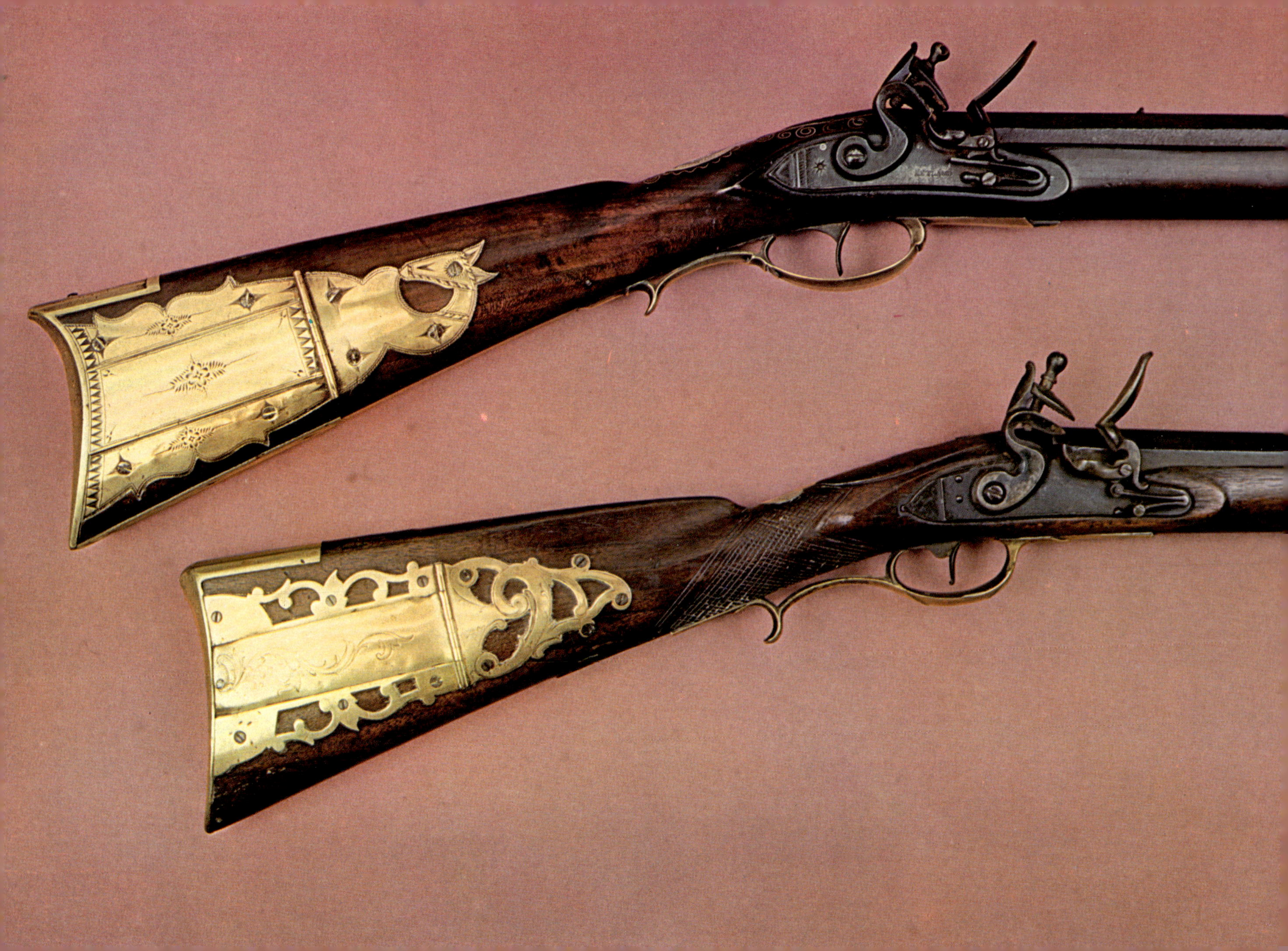

16. Regional

The Kentucky rifle reached its final, highly defined artistic form in the hands of the gunsmiths working throughout the areas of Pennsylvania here defined as schools. Within these schools, resulting from the exchange of artistic ideas, the Kentucky Rifle of the Golden Age was evolved. In the process of this evolution, Pennsylvania and Northern Maryland became the hub of a giant wheel whose spokes radiated geographically in all directions and whose rim became a great perimeter reaching as far north as Massachusetts, south to North Carolina and westward to Indiana. Within this area, the artistic influences of the Kentucky rifle made its impact on New York and the southern New England states, Maryland, Virginia and North Carolina and Kentucky, Tennessee, Ohio and Indiana. Probably nowhere within the decorative arts field did a single native product of one colony effect such a broad geographical area.

Left:

52. NEW ENGLAND. SILAS ALLEN (attributed).
The horse-headed patch box finial would make one first think of Littlestown, but this cherry-stocked rifle is as New England as they come and dates from somewhere around 1800. New England rifle authority Don Andreasen and other experts attribute this Kentucky to gunsmith Silas Allen of Shrewsbury, Massachusetts, who would have been 50 when this gun was made.

53. NEW YORK or VIRGINIA
The lower rifle on the left is signed by H. Dening. While it is a true Kentucky rifle, some of the detail such as the checkering at the wrist suggest an English rather than a Germanic background. Also, checkering as well as waterproof pans and spurred cocks were late in arriving in North America. Riflemaker Dening probably made this piece in the 1820's. The English touches suggest that Dening may have worked either in New York or Virginia but that is far from certain.

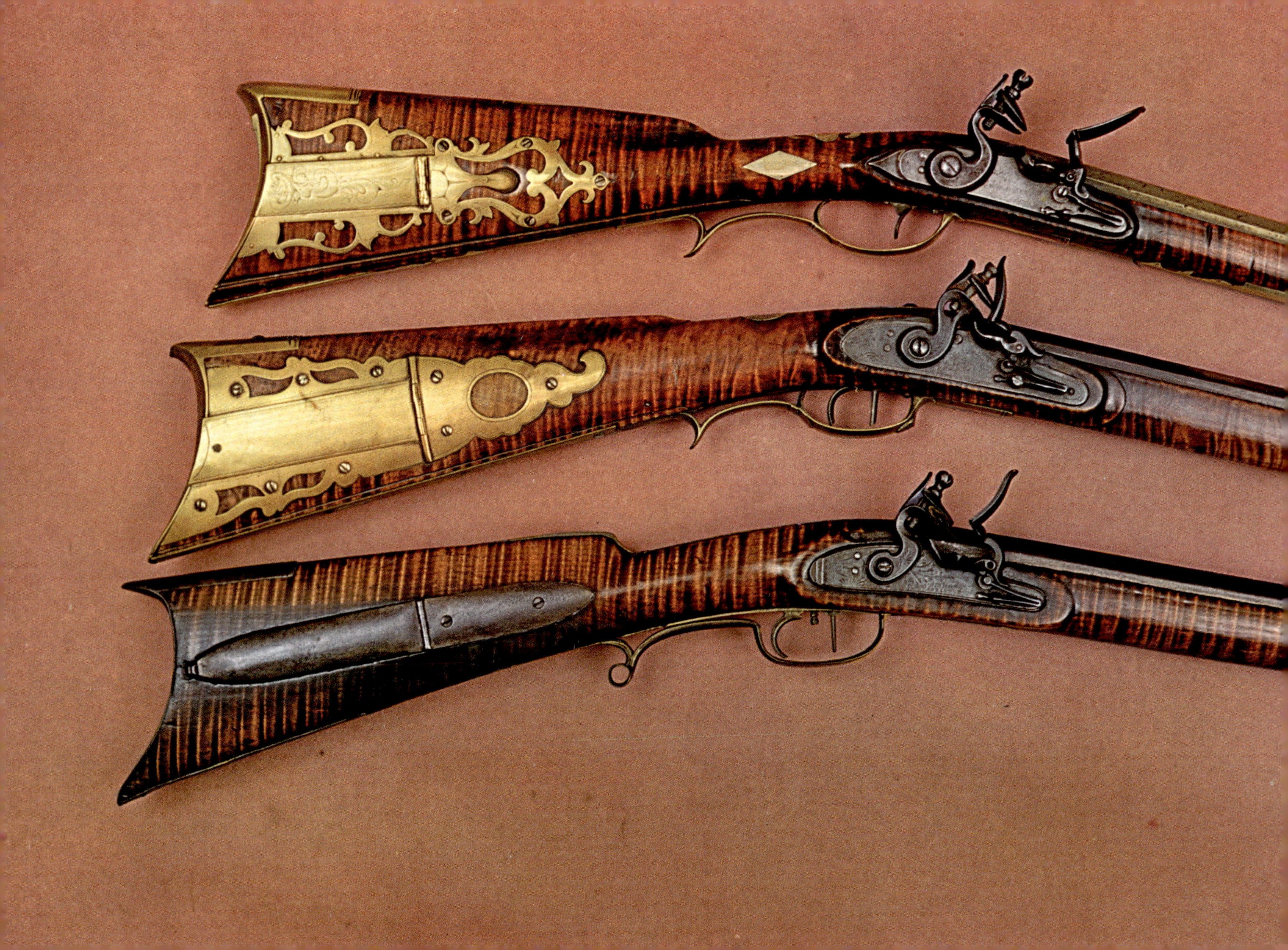

Left, top to bottom:

54. INDIANA. J. N. SMALL (signed on the barrel).
John Small began his career as a gunsmith in West Augusta, Virginia, where he is known to have been working on the eve of the American Revolution in 1775. When the war ended, he moved west to Vincennes, Indiana, where he was established as a merchant and gunsmith by 1788. Having survived the war in Virginia, his military experience led him to become a captain of the local militia. He also served as sheriff of Knox County where Vincennes is located. He continued making firearms until his death in 1821. This fine rifle with its elaborate pierced silver and brass inlays is signed on the barrel "Jn Small Vincennes" and was probably made in the years around 1800. The stock architecture of this gun, shown top left and to the right, is reminiscent of the workmanship of gunsmiths in the southwestern part of Virginia and North Carolina, where Small learned his trade. The mixture of brass and silver decoration, the formality of the urn inlay on the left side and the silver diamond on either side of the wrist reflect Small's geographical background.

55. OHIO. J. LAUTZENHEISER (signed on the barrel).
Many of the Pennsylvania German gunsmiths moved westward through Pittsburgh into Ohio in the years following the Revolution. J. Lautzenheiser worked as a gunsmith in Louisville, Ohio. The pierced patch box finial, a loop and hook or a "Q" backward, might indicate that Lautzenheiser once worked or learned his trade in the Bedford area of Pennsylvania, or he may have adopted and thickened the Bedford trademark, making it into an "O" for Ohio.

56. TENNESSEE. J. G. GROSS (signed on the barrel).
The bottom rifle on the left was made by J. G. Gross, a gunsmith who was born and raised in Tennessee and learned his trade there, unlike the Ohio and Indiana makers above, who brought their skills with

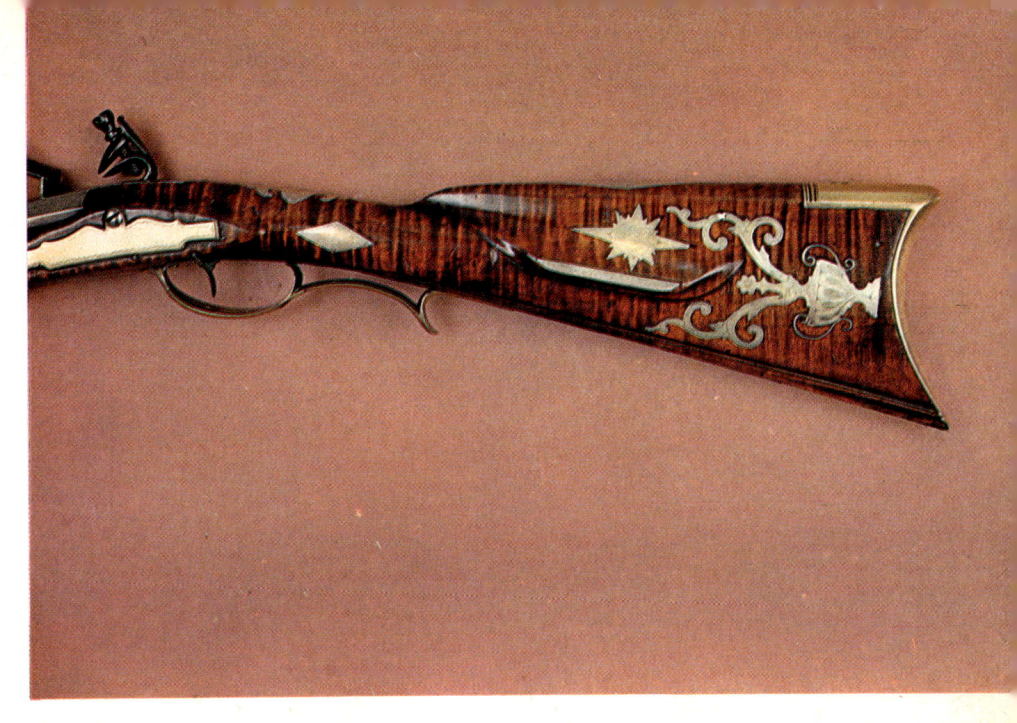

Reverse of No. 54.

them from the east. Gross was born in Tennessee in 1797 and worked at gunsmithing in Sullivan County. The rear trigger with its deep cupping and the loop at the rear of the trigger guard are the gunmaker's own ideas. The narrow iron banana-shaped patch box and, as a matter of fact, the all-iron furniture is an eastern-Tennessee-mountain characteristic. So is the long barrel tang which runs the full length of the top of the wrist, climbs to the top of the comb and continues down this ridge almost to the butt plate return. The vivid graining of the tiger maple is real and not burned in.

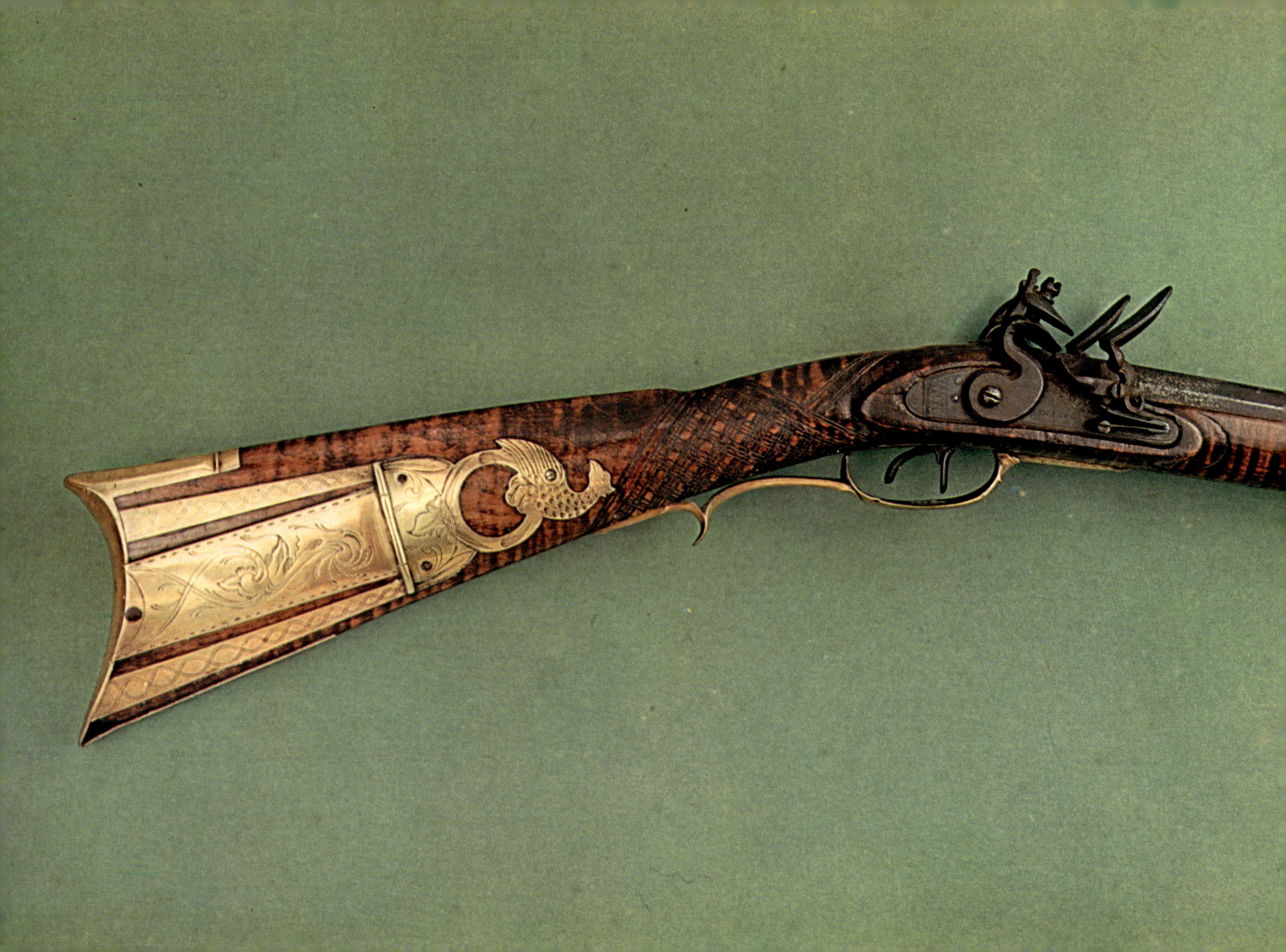

17. The Mechanism of the Kentucky

Various types of mechanisms have been tried on guns since the beginning of their invention to increase or speed up their firepower. Aside from the swivel breech over-and-under rifles, these innovations were quite late making their way into guns made in America. The elements of expense and impracticability added to curtailed production.

The over-and-under swivel breech gun was the most popular of the multi-shot rifles and was usually made with one barrel smooth and the other rifled. Occasionally you will find one with both barrels rifled; one barrel spiral rifled and the other straight cut which answers the same purpose as a smooth bore.

The swivel breech rifle in both flintlock and percussion was a practical arm that never was common but which was used as a working rifle on the frontier. Simon Kenton, the famous frontiersman of Kentucky and Ohio, ordered a swivel breech rifle from a Lancaster gunsmith in the 1770s. (See examples numbers 12, 18 & 67.)

The side-by-side was apparently next in popularity but again these are not too plentiful in rifles.

Finally, there was the rifle firing two or more shots from the same barrel. The idea was to load as many charges of powder and ball in a single barrel as you had locks for firing. This was highly impractical for frequently the flame from the first discharge would ignite the charge behind it resulting in the firing of all the charges at once.

Basically it can be said that the Kentucky rifle was slow to evolve but that the end product was totally satisfactory and that multi-shot rifles were more a curiosity than a necessity.

Left:

57. SIDE-BY-SIDE DOUBLE RIFLE

Double rifles are rare throughout the world and double-barreled shotguns, though more common, are a problem to make. (See *One Hundred Great Guns* p. 178 and following). Double-barrel flintlock guns required left- and right-hand locks and these were not easy to come by for the Kentucky rifle builder. Also, the great length of the rifle barrel made a double gun a mite muzzle heavy. For both these reasons and the need for special gunsmithing skills to make both barrels shoot to the same approximate point, the number of doubles made were few. Among those which were made during the period when the Kentucky flourished one will find various combinations of barrels. Some Kentucky doubles have two rifled barrels and some have both barrels smoothbored, while a larger percentage have one rifled and one smoothbored barrel. This later system gave the shooter maximum latitude when hunting small game. He could load the rifled barrel with ball, put shot in the smooth barrel for birds or rabbits or, if he needed a follow-up shot for a big animal such as a bear, he could put a second ball in the smooth barrel even though it shot with some loss of accuracy. A third possible combination for a double gun, which one sees most often in guns of German make, is a small bore and a large or express bored barrel either side-by-side or over-and-under. These are extremely hard to find in a Kentucky. This double rifle with its plaid checkering at the throat and pierced bird's-head patch box finial dates from the 1820s.

Right:

58. BOX-LOCK PILL-LOCK RIFLE by A. JOHNSON (signed and dated on the barrel).

According to Col. Gardner, there was an Alfred Johnson who was a gunsmith in New Geneva, Pennsylvania. This may or may not have been the man who made this gun which comes from the western part of the state. The barrel is dated 1833 which is about the cut-off date for the pill-lock type of ignition system used to fire this weapon. Percussion caps had been invented in 1818 and soon took over as the standard way to ignite a charge. Percussion powders, either loose or in pill, pellet or tube form, were all transitional between flint and true percussion or cap-lock ignition which replaced all other systems. This gun has a flat-headed hammer which crushes and detonates a nitroglycerine-sized pill of fulminating powders. The flash from this miniature explosion detonates the main charge.

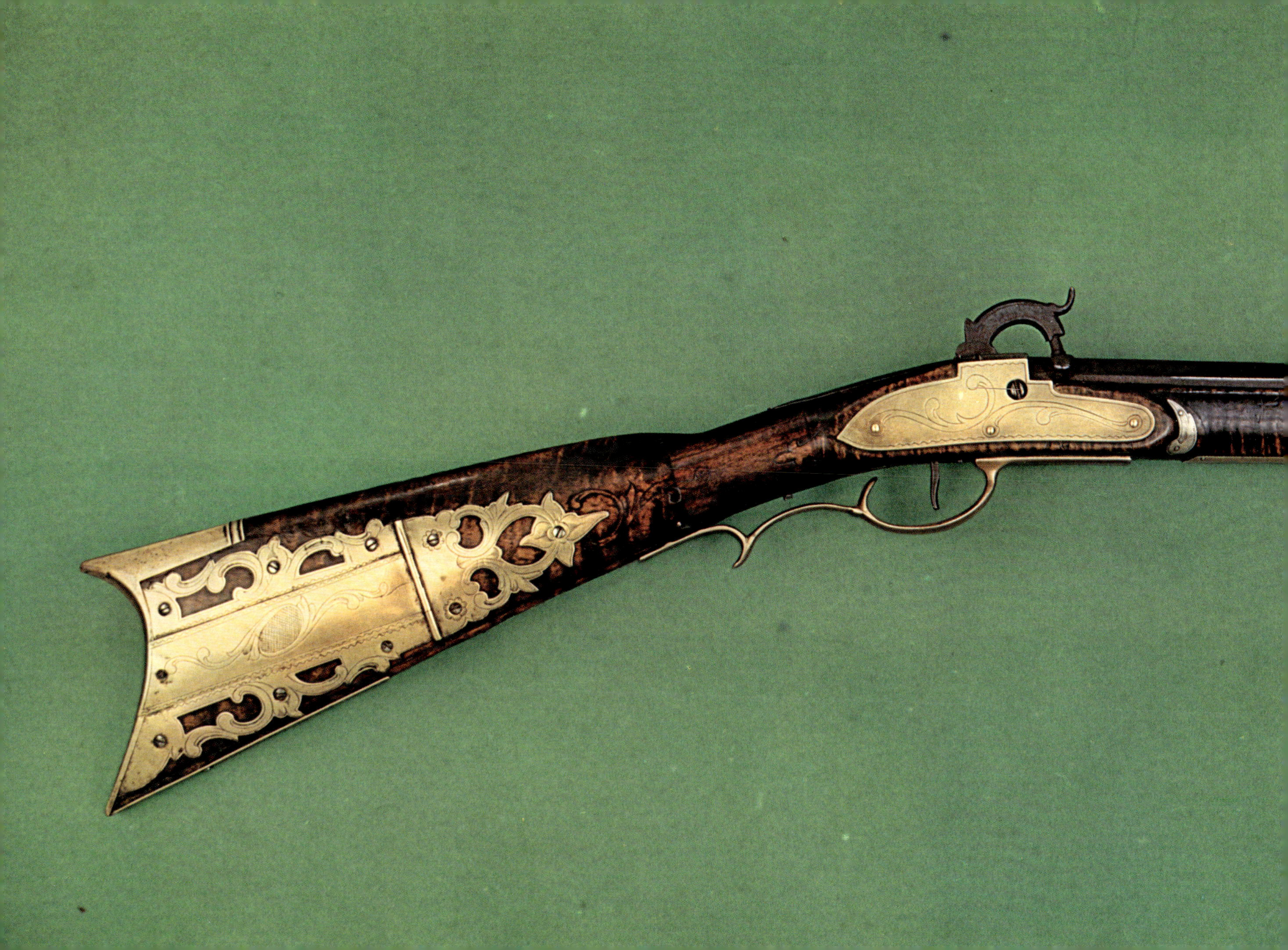

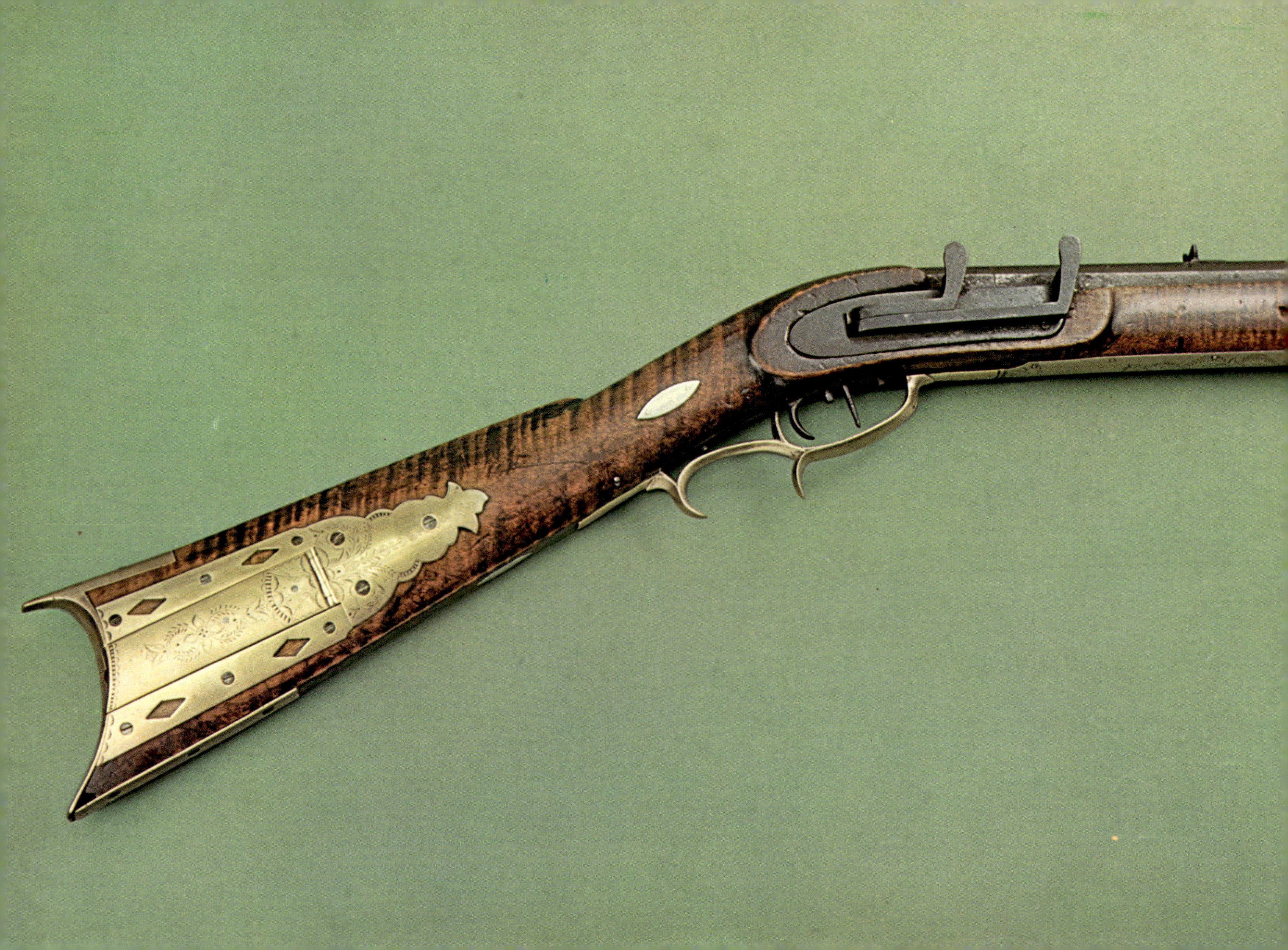

Left:

59. SUPERIMPOSED LOAD MULE-EAR PERCUSSION RIFLE

The theory has been around for a long time that you could keep pouring powder and ball down a gun barrel in layers and then shoot off one layer at a time. The facts never bore this out and many a poor sap has had his head blown off for his pains. A namesake of mine, J. P. Lindsay, was making superimposed load pistols as late as the Civil War and even sold a few to the U.S. Government, but that didn't make them any safer. According to D. R. Baxter, superimposed load firearms date back to 1360, but from then until this gun on the left was built around 1850, there are very few that have survived. One reason for their rarity is the fact that while few were built, fewer still survived being shot more than the first few times when they were nice and tight and were loaded with great care and caution. The gun pictured here and another in the Renwick Collection and one in the Winchester Gun Museum have set triggers which, when functioning properly, allowed the first mule-ear hammer to fall on the forward side mounted nipple, then on the second pull, the second hammer fell on the rear nipple. As I say, this was the theory.

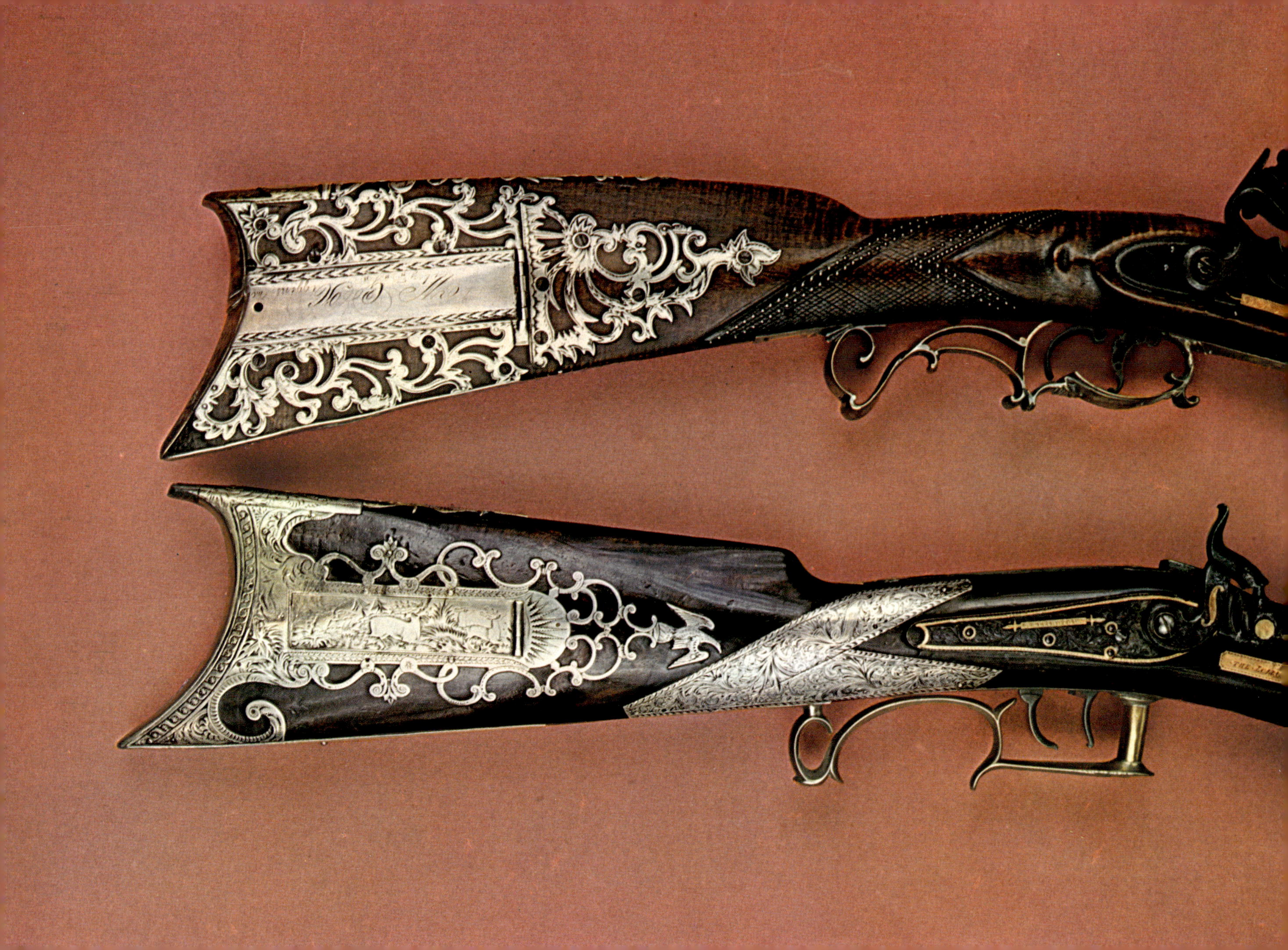

18. Silver Mounted Kentucky Rifles

Kentucky rifles fully mounted in silver or German Silver form a relatively unique category for they frequently exceed the artistic bounds of the individual gunsmith's normal work. They would appear to represent more "the presentation" piece as it is found in the case of the silversmith, the clocksmith, the potter, and the goldsmith for it generally reflects a labor of love and an effort to achieve a high degree of opulence. This is not necessarily the rifle of the frontiersman and the nation builder but the rifle made for a gentleman. Lavish silver mounted Kentucky rifles were made for presentation gifts in the years between 1830 and the Civil War.

Left, top to bottom:

60. UNKNOWN. Location unknown.
This most elaborately decorated Kentucky is more a piece of late Federal or early Victorian jewelry than it is a gun. While the double set triggers properly activate the flintlock mechanism and the piece has a rifled barrel, it is unlikely that any one ever had the heart to fire it. Because of the enormously elaborate pierced sheet silver framing of the patch box, the side plate, the left side at the butt as well as the swirling acorns and heads inlaid on the cheek, the silver nails in the throat checkering and the cast silver trigger guard, all of which are untypical, it is practically impossible to tie it down to an area or a maker. The rifle has names on it, but presumably not those of the maker. On the silver patch box lid there is the name of Wiley C. Higgins M.A. (could there have been a Master Armorer by the name

61. HARRINGTON MAKER N. YORK (signed on the lock).
The top barrel flat of this lavishly gold- and silver-mounted beauty has engraved on a gold panel insert "DAVID SHELTON, TALBOTTON, G.A. DEC. 20, 1838." This dating as well as the employment of the percussion system of ignition makes the bottom sheet silver-mounted gun anywhere from ten to fifteen years younger than the top silver-mounted piece. As you can see in the picture of the left-hand side of the gun, (top, overleaf), gold and silver has been used in alternating bands inlaid at the breech. This treatment has been used again at the muzzle and gold is inlaid in the ramrod pipes, the lock and the cast silver trigger guard. While the intent of this gun was to dazzle and not to kill, the sheet silver "V"s inlaid at the throat were a good idea. The throat was the weak point of the thin and graceful Kentucky rifle. Length overall 54¾ in., .38 cal. Loaned by the Ford Museum.

Left: Detail of barrel tops of rifles Nos. 62 & 61.

62. JACOB RUSLIN (signed on the barrel). Bedford, Somerset region, Pa.

While there were very few flintlock rifles made in the Bedford area, this piece is very clearly marked on both the barrel and lock. On the top barrel flat in Old English lettering surrounded by gold-inlaid pen flourishes in the form of feathers is the name "JACOB RUSLIN". On the flintlock lock face there is the signature of "S. Spangler", a gunsmith who is known to have worked in Somerset County. Samuel Spangler worked in Somerset County, Pa., until 1844 when he packed up and went west to become a pioneer gunsmith in Monroe, Green County, Wisconsin. This fine gun must have been made twenty years before he moved, as it is still in flint. The engraved circle segment framed silver patch box and the silver teardrop inlaid behind the lock are two of many obvious Bedford-school features of this arm. The silver patch box cover and the silver cheek piece inlays and cast silver butt plate are shown overleaf. Length overall 58⅞ in., .37 cal.

Right: Reverse of Nos. 61 & 60.

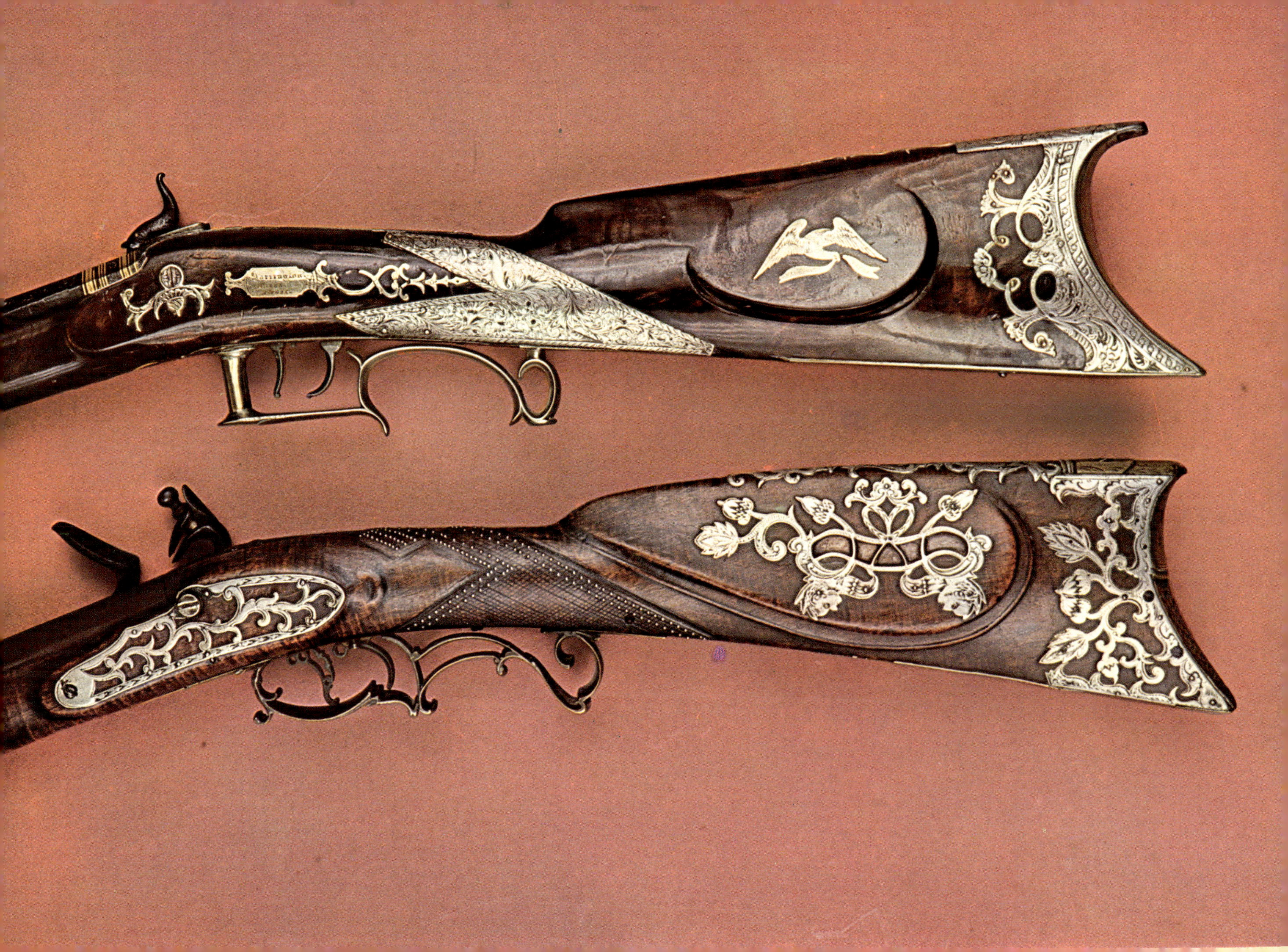

Left, top and bottom: Details of No. 62.

Right, above: Detail of No. 63. Squirrels.

63. LATE FLINT PERIOD. (1820-1835). PETER SMITH. New Berlin, Union County, Pa.

This late flintlock period starting in 1820 and continuing into the thirties saw the decline both in craftsmanship and design from the high point reached in the "Golden Age", the period around 1800. The feeling for and the use of rococo forms was lost, although some of the shapes were unknowingly retained, as they were used for silver and brass inlays. As we have noted, stock architecture degenerated as the stocks became narrow, thin and board like. There is still some shaping and carving in this piece by Peter Smith, the traditional acorns are here accompanied by a folk-art squirrel—what else? A stylized sturgeon swims down the forestock and a jumble of moons and meaningless silver inlays clutter at the wrist and around the barrel tang.

Right, below: Detail of No. 63. Fish.

Left: Detail of No. 64. Hound and rabbit.

64. PERCUSSION ERA. (1830-1870). N. A. McCOMAS, Baltimore, Md.

Nicholas McComas and his brother Alexander were both gunsmiths in Baltimore in the 19th century. Nicholas built fancy Kentuckys such as this one, while his brother made pistols, rifles and combination rifle-shotguns. Nicholas set up shop at 44 West Pratt Street in Baltimore in 1853 and was still listed as a gunsmith at that address in 1860 at the eve of the Civil War. This rifle with its copious sheet silver inlays is typical but a lot fancier than most American arms of the period. It is an aesthetic mistake. It is not really folk art, nor is it realism.

Right: Details of No. 64.

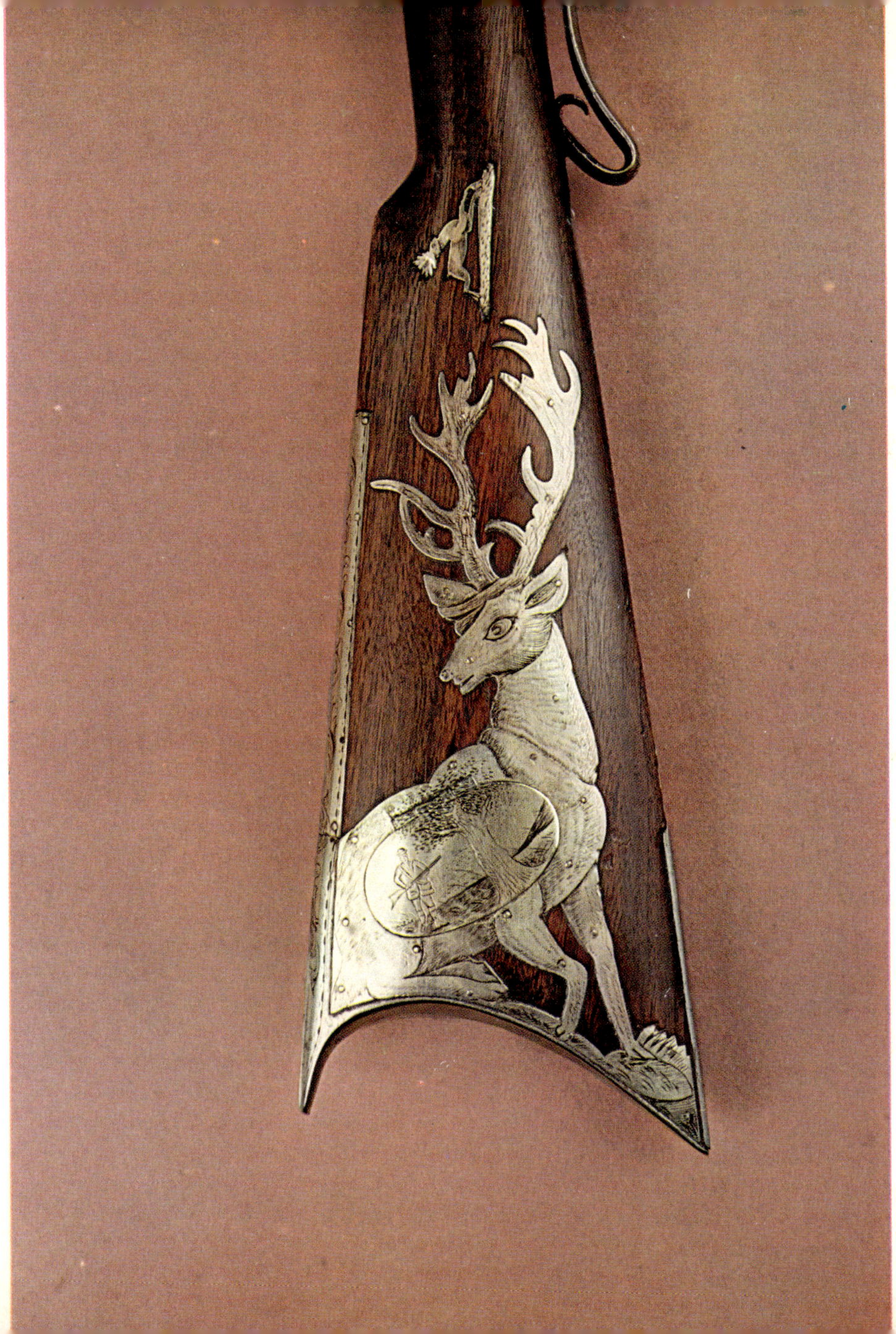
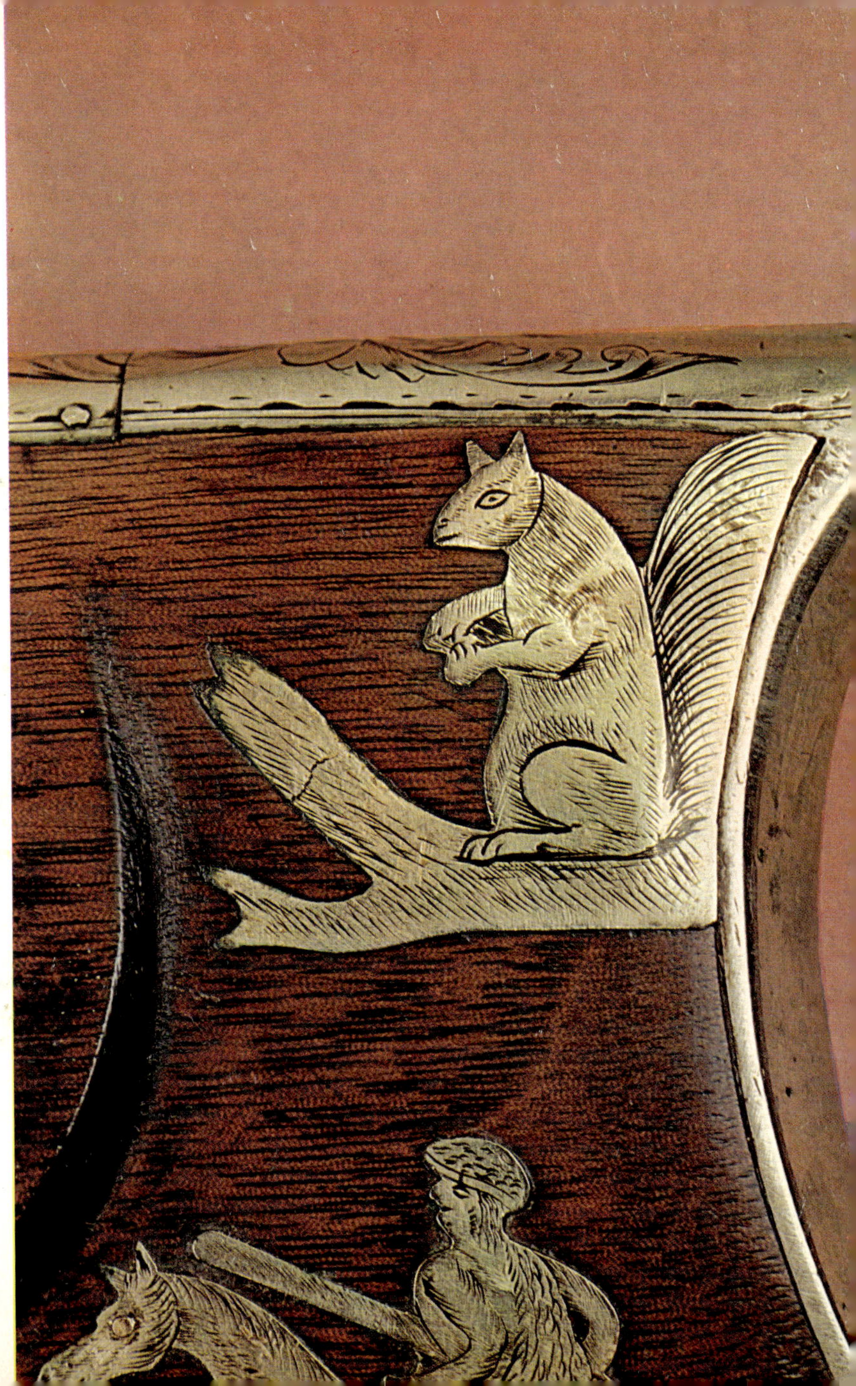

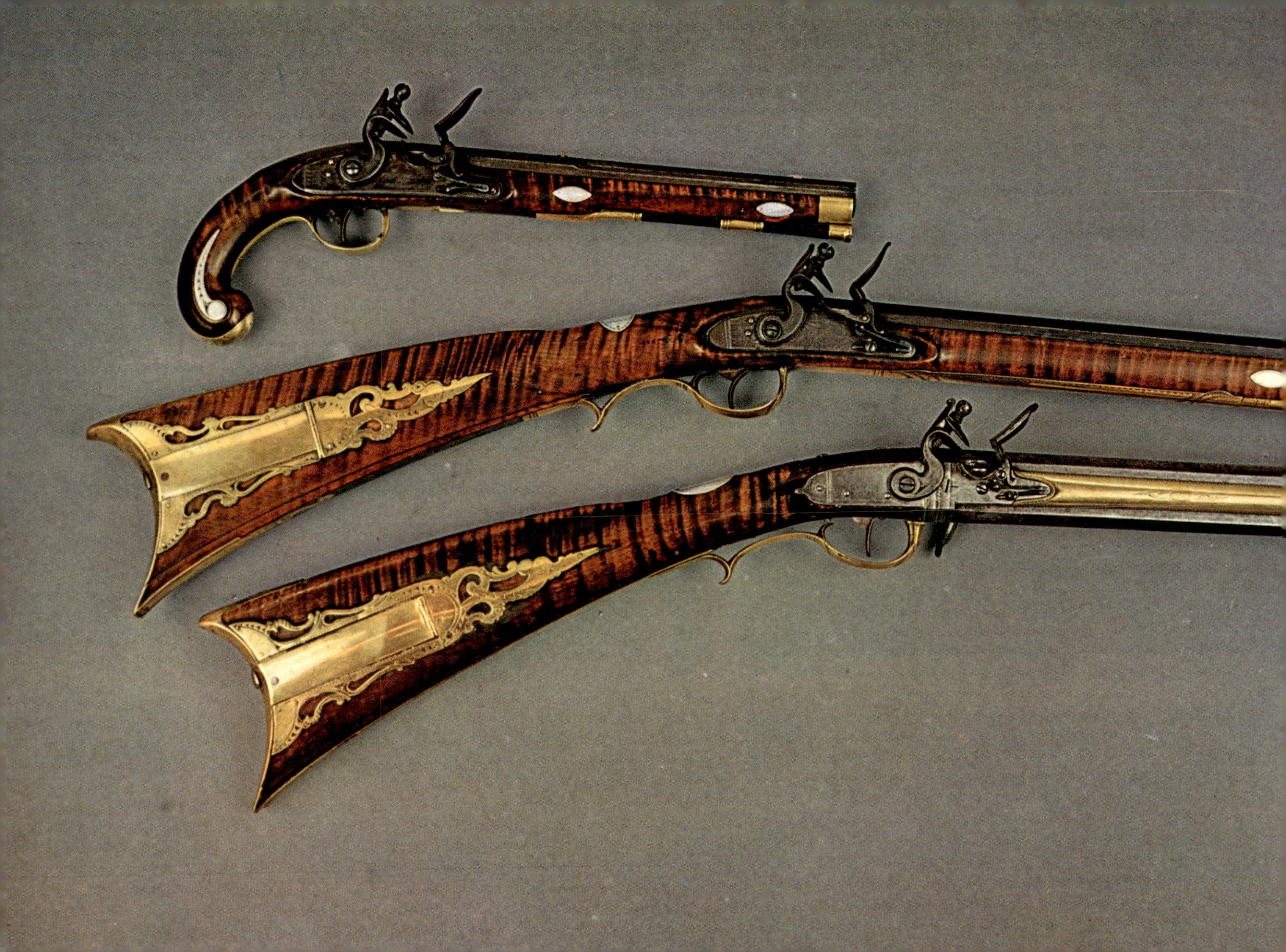

19. A Kentucky Garniture

Nicholas Hawk worked in Gilbert, Monroe County, Pennsylvania and produced guns noted for their slenderness and beauty. This suite of guns shows the range of his work—rifles, swivel breech rifle, and pistol—and is unusual not only for the condition of the pieces but also in that all three are in original flintlock condition. These pieces have not come down in time together, having been assembled as a suite by a determined collector, but it is possible that such a group might have been made at one time or another for a particular patron.

Opposite, top to bottom:

65. PISTOL. NICHOLAS HAWK (on top of the barrel). Gilbert, Monroe County, Pa.

This is a fine Kentucky pistol with ten silver inlays in the stock plus silver bands, sight and name plate inlaid in the blued barrel. The name plate reads "Nicholas Hawk". There is also an ivory inlay in the front flat portion of the trigger guard which is itself inlaid in the bottom of the stock. This one, which cannot be seen in the photograph, is heart shaped. Length overall 15 3/16 in., bbl. 10 1/16 in., .45 cal., rifled.

66. RIFLE. NICHOLAS HAWK (inlaid on top barrel flat). Gilbert, Monroe County, Pa.

What makes this group of guns a garniture is the similarity of the patch box hardware on the two long guns. The pointed finial repeats but is not identical. A signature of Hawk is a man's face cut in the brass below the point. Other Nicholas Hawk touches which are repeated on the two guns are the deeply curved butt plates, the big brass patch box door release buttons and, on the other side of the pieces, there are inlaid silver ovals in the cheeks engraved with the Lehigh Valley flattened eight-pointed star. This particular rifle has a strip of ivory inlaid to accent the shape of the cheek piece. There is an engraved comb plate and a full length floor plate on the fore end, a device often employed to cover a hole when the drill, cutting the ramrod hole, ran off. Hawk's signature is on a fancy engraved name plate inlaid in the top barrel flat. Length overall 54 3/8 in., bbl. 38 7/8 in., .44 cal., rifled.

67. SWIVEL-BREECH RIFLE. NICHOLAS HAWK GUNSMITH (barrel inlay). Gilbert, Monroe County, Pa.

This Hawk wender is a well balanced gun and not too heavy considering the over and under steel barrels. There is a brass housing along one side of the barrels which holds the ramrod. The over and under barrels are released for rotation by a second trigger ahead of the guard which retracts a spring-loaded pin from the breech of the bottom side barrel. You can't see the cheek piece, which is similar to the rifle above, or the engraved brass toe plate which runs the full length from butt plate to trigger guard extension. Hawk's name and profession are engraved on a brass barrel inlay. Length overall 54 1/2 in., bbl. 38 3/8 in., .41 cal., rifled and .43 cal., smoothbore.

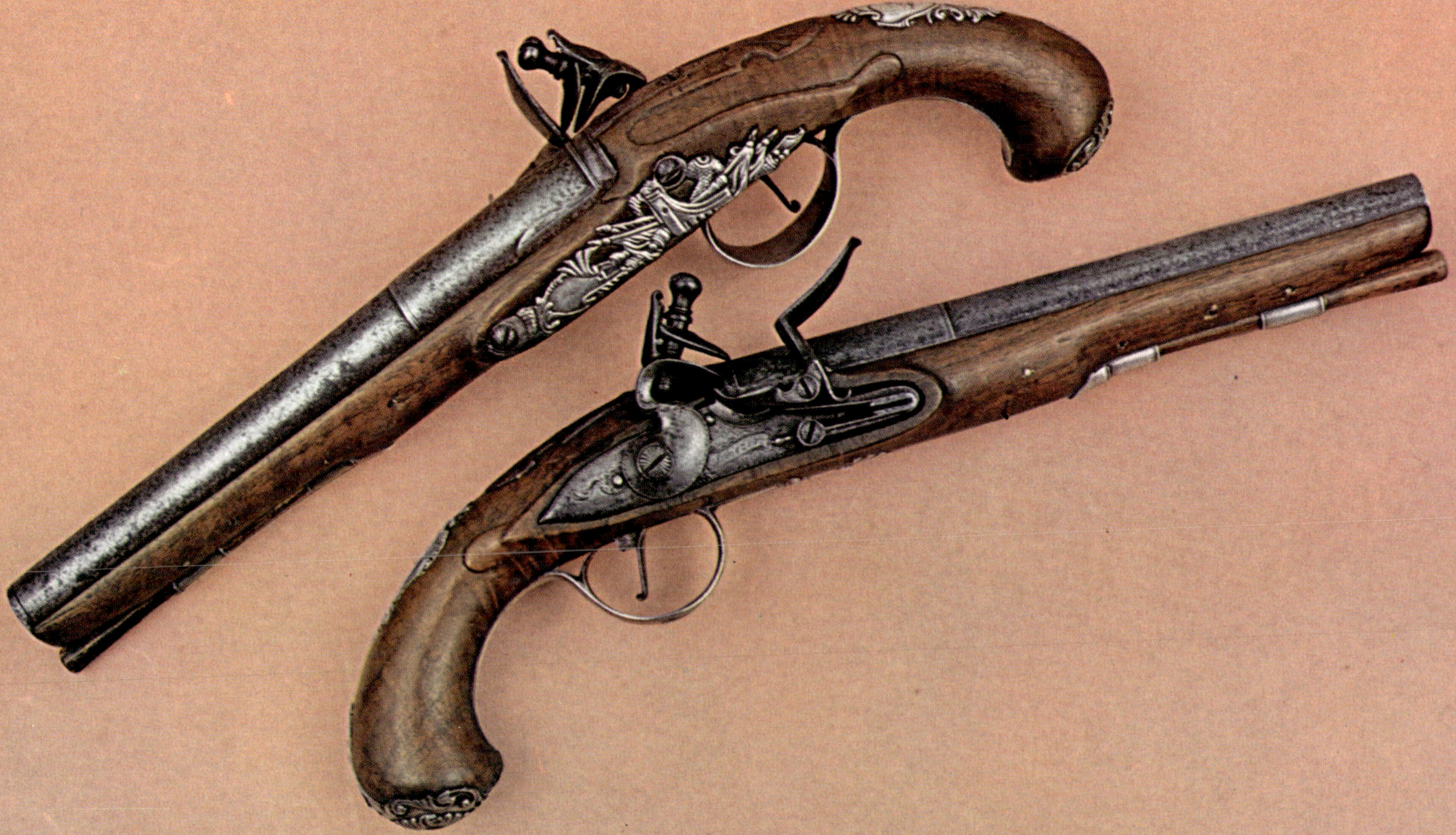

20. Kentucky Pistols

There is a great deal still to be learned about the Kentucky pistol. Whereas a large number of rifles by a given gunsmith may be available for study or examples exist that can be accurately ascribed to him, the same is not true of Kentucky pistols. Many makers are not represented by examples at all and there are no great number by any one maker. They were a luxury of the period and there are only isolated examples upon which rich ornamentation was lavished of the type expected on the finer rifles. The quality of the Kentucky pistols ranges from a large majority of extremely plain unadorned pieces to a very small handful which are exact copies of the finer class of English military pistols, even to the walnut of their stocking. We are fortunate in being able to illustrate five pairs of high quality Kentucky pistols.

Left:

68 & 69. JOHN SWITZER (engraved on the locks and barrels). Lancaster County, Pa.

The panoply cast in silver for the side plates and the cast silver butts and escutcheons could be British or European, but the pistols are very much American in the shape and treatment of the walnut stocks. Of course, it helps to know that Switzer worked in Lancaster, where he died in 1788. The smoothbored barrels are .58 calibre.

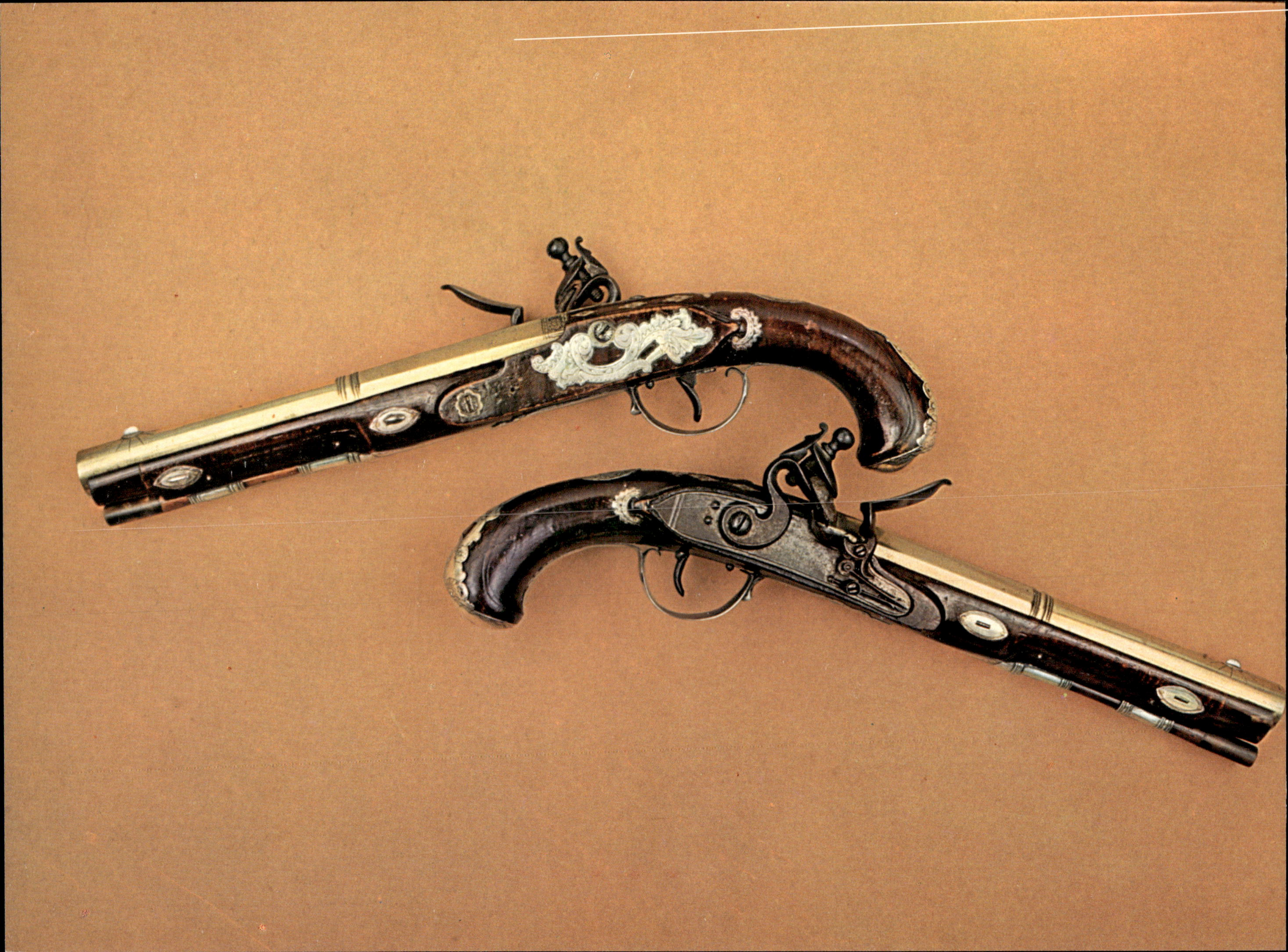

Left:

70 & 71. TOBIAS GRUBB (signed on the brass barrels). Northampton Township, Lehigh County, Pa.

This pair of Kentucky pistols on the left have sheet silver work which is *en suite* with silver work on rifles. Mother-of-pearl and horn inlays have been used as well as the silver on side plates, pistol butts, thumb, barrel slide retainers, ramrod thimbles, etc. The brass barrels are .42 calibre smoothbore.

Right, above:

72 & 73. HAMAKER (signed on the barrels). Philadelphia (?), Pa.

These fine presentation pistols are clean-lined and graceful. The simple flat silver surfaces and silver wire inlays work well with the tiger maple stocks. These silver mounted pistols were built around 1810 and equipped with imported Ketland locks. The inscription says that they were presented by Major William Watts of Humphry's Brigade, First Pennsylvania Riflemen to his adjutant W. W. K. Davis. .45 cal., smoothbore.

Right, below:

74 & 75. BEEMAN (signed on the barrels). Massachusetts.

Beeman, whose first name is unknown, was a Committee of Safety gunsmith in 1775-76. He made these pistols around 1815. One of the locks by Earps and McMain has been converted to percussion. .40 cal., smoothbore.

Overleaf:

76 & 77. PETER WHITE (initials "P.W." on barrels and locks). Uniontown, Pa.

Sheet silver mounts and hand-forged locks in the Bedford tradition, mounted on nicely marked maple stocks, make these a great pair of Kentucky pistols of the late flintlock (1825) period.

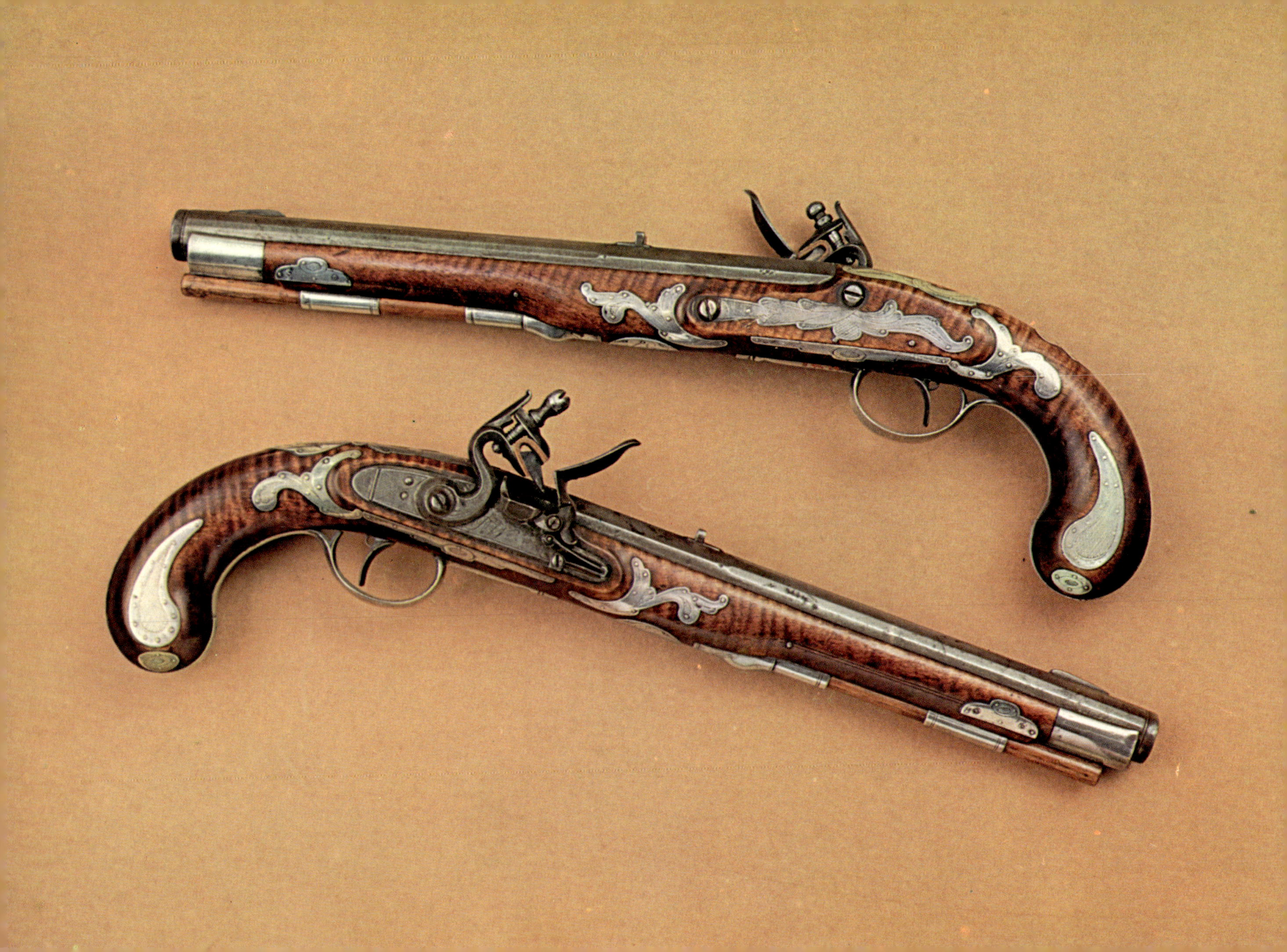

21. Gunsmiths Whose Work is Illustrated

See maker under chapter and number indicated. The dates are taken from signed pieces or indicate the period of known productivity of the gunsmith unless otherwise noted.

SILAS ALLEN (c. 1800), Shrewsbury, Mass.
REGIONAL 52

AMOS, BORDER & CO., JOHN AMOS (b. 1800–d. 1867), Bedford, Pa.
BEDFORD 38

ADAM ANGSTADT (c. 1800-1810), Kutztown, Maxatawny Township, Berks County, Pa.
ASSOCIATED BETHLEHEM 18

JOHN ARMSTRONG (1808-1841), Emmitsburg and Shields, Md.
EMMITSBURG 31 & 32, MARYLAND 41

CHRISTIAN BECK (c. 1787-1843?), Bethel and Chambersburg, Pa.
CHAMBERSBURG 35 & 36

JOHN PHILIP BECK (c. 1760-1811), Lebanon, Pa.
PRE-REVOLUTIONARY 4, LEBANON 19

BEEMAN (c. 1776-1815), Massachusetts.
PISTOLS 74 & 75

PETER BERRY (1770-1795), Heidelberg and Annville Townships, Pa.
DAUPHIN 21

NICHOLAS BEYER (1807-1815), Annville Township, Pa.
LEBANON 20

JOHN BONEWITZ (1779-1809), Womelsdorf, Heidelberg, Berks County, Pa.
READING 14

DANIEL B. BORDER (see Amos) (b. 1826–d. 1891), Bedford, Pa.
BEDFORD 38

WILLIAM DEFIBAUGH (b. 1814-d. 1891), Bedford, Pa.
BEDFORD 39

H. DENING, New York? Virginia?
REGIONAL 53

JACOB DICKERT (b. 1740-d. 1822), Manheim Township and Lancaster, Pa.
LANCASTER 5

GEORGE EISTER (b. 1762–d. 1831), Manchester Township, Pa.
YORK 25

ADAM ERNST (1800-1857), Berwick and Franklin, Pa.
YORK 24

JACOB FERREE (c. 1780-1807), Strasburg Township and Lancaster, Pa.
LANCASTER 6

MELHIOR FORDNEY (worked 1810-1846), Lancaster, Pa.
LANCASTER 7

J. G. GROSS (b. 1797), Sullivan County, Tenn.
REGIONAL 56

J. GROVE (1790-1800), Hagerstown, Md.
MARYLAND 40

TOBIAS GRUBB (c. 1800), Northhampton Township, Lehigh County, Pa.
PISTOLS 70 & 71

J. HAMAKER (c. 1810), Pennsylvania.
PISTOLS 72 & 73

HARRINGTON (1838), New York
SILVER MOUNTED 61

NICHOLAS HAWK (1782-1844), Gilbert, Monroe County, Pa.
GARNITURE 65, 66 & 67

CHRISTIAN HUFFMAN (1782-1805), Woodstock, Va.
VIRGINIA 44

A. JOHNSON (1833), Western Pa.
MECHANISM 58

F. KLETTE (c. 1770), Stevensburg, Va.
VIRGINIA 47

JACOB KUNTZ (1799-1811), Lehigh, Lehigh County & Philadelphia, Pa.
BETHLEHEM 12

SIMON LAUCK (1806 was the year of the eclipse), Winchester, Va.
VIRGINIA 43

J. LAUTZENHEISER, Louisville, Ohio.
REGIONAL 55

N. A. McCOMAS (1853-1860), 44 Pratt St., Baltimore, Md.
SILVER MOUNTED 64

J. MONTAGUE (c. 1800), Winchester, Va.
VIRGINIA 46

PETER NEIHART (c. 1787), Whitehall Township, Lehigh County, Pa.
BETHLEHEM 8 & 11

JOHN NOLL (1800-1820), Washington Township, Franklin County, Pa.
CHAMBERSBURG 34

HENRY PICKEL (1780-1800), York, Pa.
YORK 22

LEONARD REEDY (1792-1837), Gratz, Dauphin County, Pa.
READING 15

NATHANIEL ROWE (c. 1800-1860), Emmitsburg, Md.
EMMITSBURG 33

HERMAN RUPP (1784-1809), Macungie Township, Lehigh, Pa.
BETHLEHEM 9 & 10

JACOB RUSLIN (1825), Bedford-Somerset region, Pa.
SILVER MOUNTED 62

JOHN SCHNEIDER (1776), (Location unknown).
PRE-REVOLUTIONARY 2

GEORGE SCHREYER (1767-1813), Hanover, Pa.
EMMITSBURG 30 & YORK 26

JOHN SCHREIT (1761-1768), Reading, Pa.
PRE-REVOLUTIONARY 1

FREDERICK SELL (b. 1781?-d. 1869?), Littlestown, Pa.
LITTLESTOWN 28

JACOB SELL, THE YOUNGER (b. 1780-d. 1855), Littlestown, Pa.
LITTLESTOWN 29

JACOB SHAFFER (1825-1835), Wythe County, Va.
    VIRGINIA 45

JOHN SHRIVER (1793-1801), Adams County, Pa.
    LITTLESTOWN 27

JOHN SMALL (1775-1821), Vincennes, Indiana.
    REGIONAL 54

PETER SMITH (1820-1835), New Berlin, Union County, Pa.
    SILVER MOUNTED 63

JACOB STOUDENOUR (1795-1863), Colerain Township, Bedford, Pa.
    BEDFORD 37

FREDERICK STOVER (c. 1800-1826), Emmitsburg School.
    MARYLAND 42

JOHN SWITZER (1770-1788), Lancaster County, Pa.
    PISTOLS 68 & 69

A. VERNER (1770-1790), Bucks County, Pa.
    ASSOCIATED BETHLEHEM 17

NATHANIEL VOGLER (1804-1850), Salem, N.C.
    NORTH CAROLINA 49

PETER WHITE (c. 1825), Uniontown, Pa.
    PISTOLS 76 & 77

JOHN YOUNG (c. 1800), Easton, Pa.
    BETHLEHEM 13

FREDERICK ZORGER (b. 1734-d. 1815), Newberry, York County, Pa.
    YORK 23

Manufactured by LIBREX, Milan, Italy